GW00482007

COUNTRY HOUSES OF THE COTSWOLDS

COUNTRY HOUSES OF THE COTSWOLDS

Nicholas Mander

AURUM

First published in Great Britain 2008 by Aurum Press Limited
7 Greenland Street, London NW1 0ND
www.aurumpress.co.uk

A catalogue record for this book is available from the British Library.
ISBN 978 1 84513 331 3

10 9 8 7 6 5 4 3 2 1
2012 2011 2010 2009 2008

Design by James Campus
Originated, printed and bound in Singapore by C S Graphics

Frontispiece: *Kelmscott Manor, Oxfordshire.*

THE COUNTRY LIFE PICTURE LIBRARY

The *Country Life* Picture Library holds a complete set of prints made from its negatives, and a card index to the subjects, usually recording the name of the photographer and the date of the photographs catalogued, together with a separate index of photographers. It also holds a complete set of *Country Life* and various forms of published indices to the magazine. The Library may be visited by appointment, and prints of any negatives it holds can be supplied by post.

For further information, please contact the Library Manager, Justin Hobson, at *Country Life*, Blue Fin Building, 110 Southwark Street, London SE1 0SU (*Tel: 020 3148 4474*).

ACKNOWLEDGEMENTS

Firstly my thanks are due to Jeremy Musson, former architectural editor of *Country Life*, who set this project in motion and nursed it through to publication, for his unstinting encouragement and guidance; also to my late friends, predecessors, colleagues, David Verey, Norman Jewson and James Lees-Milne.

I thank the owners and their stewards past and present for their courtesy in showing and sharing their houses, and their hospitality in matters great and small. I would thank particularly HRH The Prince of Wales, Guy Acloque, Lord Apsley, Lady Ashcombe, the Duke and Duchess of Beaufort, Major John Berkeley, Simon Biddulph, Michael Claydon, Henry Elwes, John Evetts, Christine Facer, David Lowsley-Willliams, Lady Killearn, Thomas and Penelope Messel, Cullum McAlpine, John Milne, Lord Neidpath, Dr Edward Peake, the Marquis Nicholas de Piro, Mrs Laurence Rook, Erica Mary Sanford, Roger Seelig, Nick and Kai Spencer, the Hon. Philip Smith, Jenny Stringer, and the late Charles Wingfield. Among many others who have been generous with their time and scholarship are Jean Bray, Stephen Davis, Martin Drury, John Harris, Jeffrey Haworth, Richard Hewlings, Michael Hill, Nicholas Kingsley, Anthony and Dr Brigitte Mitchell, Paul Moir, Dr Alan Powers, Dr John Martin Robinson, Dr Kirsty Rodwell and Rory Young. My wife, Karin, has shared in the joy of many discoveries, above all that of our own magical house, where she continues to keep up the family motto: *vive bene*.

Finally, I remember my late parents, who by chance first introduced me to so many owners and their houses nearly fifty years ago: it is to their memories therefore that I dedicate this book.

This book is in every sense a collaboration. Clare Howell, my tactful editor, has been an unfailing source of inspiration, with a sharp eye for detail, and unflappable patience, where deadlines and space were always very tight. James Campus has designed the book and laid out the incomparable photographs from the archive of *Country Life* with dedication and inventive artistry, and helped hone difficult choices. Justin Hobson and his staff at the *Country Life* Picture Library have been exemplary, readily hunting down the obscurest missing photographs. The photographs speak for themselves. All errors of attribution and fact are entirely my own.

LIST OF ARTICLES

This is a list of the primary articles in *Country Life* for which the photographs reproduced in this book were taken. The photographer's name has been given in brackets, where known.

Abbotswood, Gloucestershire: 22 February 1913.
Angeston Grange, Gloucestershire: 1 March 2001 (Paul Barker).
Alderley Grange, Gloucestershire: 9 October 1969 (Alex Starkey).
Badminton House, Gloucestershire: 14 September 1907; 1 December 1929; 25 November 1934; 4 April 1968.
Asthall Manor, Gloucestershire: 29 June 1945 (A. E. Henson).
Barnsley House, Gloucestershire: 26 September1974 (Alex Starkey).
Barnsley Park, Gloucestershire: 2 May 1908; 2 and 9 September 1954 (A. E. Henson).
Batsford Park, Gloucestershire: 4 July 1903.
Beacon House, Gloucestershire: 21 April 1916; 17 October 1996 (June Buck).
Berkeley Castle, Gloucestershire: 29 July and 16 August 1916; 4, 11 and 18 June 1932 (Arthur Gill); 4 February 1933.
Beverston Castle, Gloucestershire: 18 and 25 February 1944.
Bibury Court, Gloucestershire: 7 September 1912; 16 May 1931.
Bradley Court, Gloucestershire: 15 September 2005 (Will Pryce).
Burford Priory, Oxfordshire: 4 March 1911; 3 and 10 June 1939 (A. E. Henson); 31 December 1981.
Campden House, Chipping Campden, Gloucestershire: 18 February 1999 (Paul Barker).
Castle Godwyn, Gloucestershire: 27 September 2007 (Will Pryce).
Chastleton House, Oxfordshire: 19 July 1902; 25 January and 1 February 1919; 18 June 1998 (Paul Barker).
Chavenage House, Gloucestershire: 15 April 1911; 1 May 2003 (Paul Barker).
Cirencester House, Gloucestershire: 8 August 1908; 16 and 23 June 1950 (Westley); 7 January 1960.
Cold Ashton Manor, Gloucestershire: 14 and 21 February 1925 (A. E. Henson).
Daneway House, Gloucestershire: 6 March 1909; 1 December 1934; 4 January 1952; 28 September 2006 (Paul Barker).
Dixton Manor, Gloucestershire: 26 April and 3 May 1946.
Dodington Park, Gloucestershire: 2 February 1924 (Ward); 13 January 1955; 22 and 29 November 1956.
Doughton Manor, Gloucestershire: 13 May 1905; 26 November 1943 (Westley).
Down Ampney House, Gloucestershire: 27 October 1917.
Dyrham Park, Gloucestershire: 26 September 1903; 14 November 1916; 13 October 1988.
Eyford House, Gloucestershire: 15 March 1924; 7 October 2004 (Paul Barker).
Hidcote Manor, Gloucestershire: 22 February 1930 (A. E. Henson).
Highgrove House, Gloucestershire: 14 May 1998 (June Buck).
Hilles, Gloucestershire: 7 and 14 September 1940 (A. E. Henson).
Iron Acton Court, Gloucestershire: 28 March 1908.
Kelmscott Manor, Oxfordshire: 20 and 27 August 1921 (A. E. Henson); 3 January 1947; 28 May 1992 (Julian Nieman); 24 November 2005 (Paul Barker).
The Leasowes, Gloucestershire: 6 March 1909; 3 January 1947.
Little Sodbury Manor, Gloucestershire: 7 October 1922 (Ward).
Lodge Park, Gloucestershire: 18 May 2000 (Paul Barker).
Lypiatt Park, Gloucestershire: 1 December 1900; 9 July 1964.
Nether Lypiatt Manor, Gloucestershire: 31 March and 7 April 1923 (F. Sleigh); 19 and 26 May 1934 (A. E. Henson); 24 November 2005.
Nether Swell Manor, Gloucestershire: 26 November 1910.
Newark Park, Gloucestershire: 3 October 1985 (Jonathan M. Gibson).
Owlpen Manor, Gloucestershire: 11 January 1913; 6 October 1906; 2 and 9 November 1951 (A. E. Henson); 28 September 2000 (Paul Barker).
Painswick House, Gloucestershire: 1 September 1917; 13 February 1992; 18 February and 15 July 1993 (Garden Picture Library).
Pinbury Park, Gloucestershire: 30 April 1910.
Poulton Manor, Gloucestershire: 27 May 1976 (Jonathan M. Gibson).
Prinknash Park, Gloucestershire: 22 September 1906.
Rodmarton Manor, Gloucestershire: 4 April 1931 (Arthur Gill and Westley); 19 and 25 October 1978 (Alex Starkey).
Sezincote House, Gloucestershire: 13 and 20 May 1939 (A. E. Henson); 2 September 1976 (Jonathan M. Gibson); 9 June 1977 (Jonathan M. Gibson); 10 January 2002 (Melanie Eclare).
Snowshill Manor, Gloucestershire: 1 October 1927 (F. Sleigh); 18 May 1978 (Findlay Davidson); 17 April 1980 (Alex Starkey); 15 December 1988 (Alex Starkey).
Stanton Court, Gloucestershire: 25 November 1911.
Stanway House, Gloucestershire: 1 July 1899; 25 November 1916; 3, 10 and 17 December 1964 (Alex Starkey).
Stout's Hill, Gloucestershire: 5 July 1973 (Alex Starkey).
Sudeley Castle, Gloucestershire: 23, 30 November and 7 December 1940 (A. E. Henson); 5 October 1961.
Upper Dorvel House, Gloucestershire: 10 April 1909.
Waverton House, Gloucestershire: 6 August 1981 (Charles Hall).
Westonbirt House, Gloucestershire: 18 March 1905; 18 and 25 May 1972 (Jonathan M. Gibson).
Woodchester Park, Gloucestershire: 6 February 1969 (Alex Starkey); 1 June 1989 (Keith Hewitt).
Wormington Grange, Gloucestershire: 21 September 1940 (A. E. Henson); 20 and 28 October 1988.

CONTENTS

✲

THE COTSWOLD MANOR HOUSE and its setting assumed iconic status in the late nineteenth and early twentieth centuries. At its most potent, it became a symbol of Edwardian nationalism, of the enduring values of 'Old English' civilisation itself, and of the unquestioned legitimacy of a benevolent gentry class whose values were rooted in the land. This ideal was fostered from the start by *Country Life*, which was founded in 1897, and the magazine occupies a central place as a pioneer interpreter and forceful advocate of the Cotswold house and its landscape.

Country Life

Inspired by the dominant critique of William Morris, who urged the revival of vernacular styles, *Country Life* did much to discover and popularise the Cotswolds and to raise its fine houses to cult status. The first issues of the magazine featured early manor houses, such as Chavenage, Chastleton, Stanway, Owlpen, Burford Priory, Cold Ashton Manor, and Daneway, some of them houses little known at that time, which reflected the emphasis of Edwardian taste on the Arcadian setting, the authentic surface, and the unrestored 'Tudor-bethan' interior. Under the influence of architects such as Norman Shaw, Philip Webb and later Sir Edwin Lutyens, the appeal broadened to include the Georgian vernacular of houses like Nether Lypiatt and Lyegrove. After a thousand weekly numbers, a retrospective editorial in March 1916 defined the sort of house admired by the readers of *Country Life*: 'some are remarkable for their homely charm, others for their stately dignity; some excel from the delight of their surrounding gardens, others from the perfection of their interior decorations.'

Contributions established a pervasive mood of antiquarian nostalgia, descriptive rather than critical, perfunctory on architectural history, with digressions into fustian genealogical and manorial descents, and diffuse evocations of the romantic atmosphere of gardens and picturesque views. Yet the articles were carefully researched in the field, original accounts, delightfully presented, of their time and place, and illustrated with photographs of outstanding quality. This was developed over the following decades with a greater authority in range and depth of analysis. This formula has ensured the success of *Country Life* to this day and led to an amassing of articles and photographs, which forms the magazine's unrivalled archive and an indispensable architectural record.

Above: *Burford Priory, Burford. The late Elizabethan south front with the chapel, to the left, added by William Lenthall, Speaker of the Long Parliament, about 1662.*

Left: *Chavenage House, near Tetbury. View into the Edwardian ballroom: the chunky, stepped columns to the fireplace are by the Yorkshire architect, J. T. Micklethwaite, 1904–05.*

Cotswold landscape

The Cotswolds have never been a political or administrative territory. They are geophysical: a chain of limestone hills slanting obliquely from north east to south west, on average some twenty miles wide. Today it is generally accepted that the Cotswolds extend fifty odd miles from the mound of Meon Hill by Chipping Campden, in the north, to Lansdown Hill and St Catherine's Court (with its Elizabethan manor house), where they dip into Bath, in the south. Their heart-land is embedded in the historic county of Gloucestershire, with forays into the adjacent parts of Warwickshire, Oxford-shire (Burford to Heythrop) and (briefly) Worcestershire – where some of its most famous villages lie, like Broadway. These meet (or met) at the 'four shires' stone just east of Moreton-in-Marsh.

The landscape of the Cotswolds is varied, with escarpment, river valleys, and the upland plateau of 'high wild hills and rough uneven ways', complained of by Shakespeare's Northumberland. The scarp, known locally as the Ridge or 'Edge', is the most dramatic feature, fringed for miles with shallow-rooting beech woods on the steeper slopes, defining the Cotswolds abruptly to the west, a cliff of land with steep combes, dingles and trackless 'bottoms' (as the local word has it) where the hills weave in and out as if along the foreshore of an ancient sea. The scarp overlooks the gentle dairy country of the Severn Vale, with its contrasting timber architecture, and the Welsh hills beyond. Early houses, on medieval foundations, nestle by the spring line in many of the deep valleys, from Dyrham to Stanway. Later houses command prospects from the dry summits: Newark Park, the 'new work', is dated from the 1550s, Cold Ashton from about 1630. A few outliers resembling the Arthurian hills of Somerset lie stranded in the Severn Vale: Meon Hill, Dumbleton and Bredon, Robin's Wood, Churchdown, Cam Long Down, Coaley Peak. To the south east they shelve gently into the level clays of Oxfordshire and Wiltshire, where the hills fade bashfully, without drama or declivity.

The harmony between building and setting is the striking feature of the Cotswold landscape – where a vernacular tradition evolved robust and almost changeless from about 1450 to the Industrial Revolution. The country houses are

often ornaments to the landscape – the highlight which catches the eye. Indeed the landscape with its outstanding houses and villages has been recognised as an area of incomparable scenic interest and one of the most popular tourism regions in rural England since Victorian times. It was given protected status in 1966, when the Government designated it an Area of Outstanding Natural Beauty. After extensions in 1990, it is now the largest AONB in England at over 790 square miles, 78 miles from north to south, defining the area safeguarded as one stretching from Edge Hill in Warwickshire to the Hintons south of Bath, in Somerset.

Wool

The Cotswold sheep, whose fleeces for centuries provided the wool and so the wealth of the region, probably derive from a large polled breed introduced by the Romans, whose skeletal remains are found sporadically in the archaeological record. Their medieval descendants seen on the memorial brasses of the wool merchants appear scrawny and thin boned. Already in Michael Drayton's *Polyolbion* (1546) they were known as Cotswold 'lions', on account of their size rather than their courage, with distinctive tufted forelocks. They were improved in the eighteenth century and are today a large longwool breed, like the Border Leicester, and, having hovered on the brink of extinction for many years, there has been some revival of interest and numbers.

The Cotswold houses were based on the fortunes of wool, not only producing a commodity from the fleeces of the sheep, but trading in, or later processing, wool and textiles, ultimately in an industrial system. Tombs or more typically monumental brasses of the merchant woolmen show them standing on their sacks of wool, or with sheep as their footrests. Fulling mills are recorded at Temple Guiting by 1185. The wool was exported raw to centres in Flanders up to the thirteenth century. There are Flemish weavers recorded in Wotton-under-Edge by 1330, and by the fifteenth century much of the wool clip was being converted into cloth in England.

Then wool was woven in rural mills along the power source on the rivers. These were centred on Cirencester and Tetbury, for long wool, and the Stroud valleys, for fine broadcloth, which was produced from fulled and felted short wool. Many of the gentry houses from Chastleton to Doughton Manor and Highgrove were the homes of an interbred class of mill owners, weavers and woolmen.

By 1750 a proto-industrial revolution had taken place in the rural Cotswolds, endowed with the ready combination of wool and water. Yet, the woollen cloth industry which had been the dynamo of the local economy, after a short boom with the introduction of steam mills, collapsed definitively in the 1830s, leading to rural poverty and mass emigration, and leaving much of the region rural, poor and 'almost feudal'. The Industrial Revolution itself seemed to have bypassed the Cotswolds. Apart from a sporadic textile industry in the Stroud valleys and specialised trades, such as the blankets of Witney, and isolated agro-industrial buildings, such as the Blockley silk mills, Bliss Mills outside Chipping Norton, and Donnington Brewery, the region remained changeless countryside into the middle of the twentieth century.

Cotswold stone

The Cotswold hills are formed of limestone of the Oolite, signifying 'eggstone', because it has the texture of cods' roe. Looked at closely, it is made up of tiny skeletal globules deposited over millennia as sand dunes in the warm subtropical seas, whose shallows covered the area in the Jurassic era, about 150–200 million years ago, bonded together in a matrix of calcium carbonate.

In architectural terms Cotwold limestone conjours, perhaps, the most exquisitely versatile building material in England, giving life to a vernacular tradition which has adapted over

centuries to create one of the country's most widely admired, as well as most resilient regional styles. A broad belt of limestone shows colours and reflective tints that change in continuous gradations from deep ochre and Verona brown through the 'broken ivory of freshly-shorn sheep' to pearl grey in the south. A tinge of tawny brown makes its mark in the contrasting marlstones of Oxfordshire and Northamptonshire.

The Cotswold strata have been quarried as an excellent building material: fine grained, responsive to chisel and hammer, adaptable, durable, and when necessary delicate in its carved features and flourishes. The stone is soft when freshly quarried, carved before it weathers into the crisp defining dressings and mouldings of the Cotswold vernacular.

The stone houses of the vernacular were not left bare to the elements, as we are accustomed to seeing them today. Generally, as William Cobbett emphasised, the softer walling stone was limewashed and, in the case of the sandier, open-grained rubble of the south, rendered or 'harled'. He described the overwhelmingly *white* villages of the south Cotswolds:

Left: *Dixton Manor, near Alderton. Mainly Jacobean, it looks oddly truncated, having been reduced to a farmhouse (to the left) by Samuel Gist, of Wormington Grange, in 1795.*

Above: *Owlpen Manor, near Uley, from the south east. Tudor vernacular which has grown and adapted over three centuries to 1719. The outbuildings to the right were demolished, c.1964.*

'The houses are built with this [yellowish, ugly stone]; and, it being ugly, the stone is made *white* by a wash of some sort or other.' The strong white is killed with a hint of ochre or Sienna brown, at its best at the estate village in Badminton, for example. Rarely, as at Owlpen and Whitminster House, there is pargework incised into the plaster as the ornament of a gable end or curvilinear window detail; more often there is modelled plasterwork in the interiors (Daneway, Little Sodbury, Burford Priory, Upper Swell, Chastleton and, in the revivals of the Gimson school, at Upper Dorvel and Pinbury). It was in response to the proposed 'scraping' of Tewkesbury Abbey, threatening the loss of its lime plaster, that William Morris first founded the Society for the Protection of Ancient Buildings, still affectionately known as 'Anti-Scrape'.

Craftsmen

The fine stone and its working traditions which had evolved spontaneously on isolated farms gave rise to the organised body of craftsmen builders and master masons, working in an anonymous craft guild system, whose arcane masons' marks are scribed in the great Benedictine abbey churches of Gloucester and Tewkesbury, laicised at the Reformation, and the countless parish churches of the Cotswold hills. The

quarries became the nurseries of the masons, such as the Woodwards of Chipping Campden and the Strongs of Burford.

The names and careers of the master masons and sculptors in the early modern period are recorded, sometimes as dynasties over several generations. The Strong family, owners of quarries in Little Barrington and Taynton, are the best known, active in the Cotswolds throughout the seventeenth and early eighteenth centuries. Masons and master builders with versatile skills often worked effectively as architects, overseeing the works as executants, employed under the direct supervision of a landowner or his agent, working with their models and pattern books. The best served their apprenticeships in the metropolitan tradition and, employed in the circle of court architects, were influential in spreading a mature Classical style, which began to percolate deep into the rural Cotswolds by the late sixteenth century.

In the early twentieth century, the ideal of the architect-craftsman as the animating spirit of the structure was revived under the leaders of the Arts and Crafts movement: Ernest Gimson, Detmar Blow, the Barnsley brothers, and Norman Jewson. They worked closely with their teams of craftsmen, often as 'itinerant architects', employing them as direct labour, recording and observing their traditional skills, working methods and designs, and often adapting them to serve new uses in collaboration. They survive into our own time, where artist-craftsmen like Rory Young of Cirencester and Simon Verity, under the encouragement of his great-uncle Oliver Hill, at Daneway, have continued to make a distinctive contribution in conservation as well as original work in sculpture.

The Cotswold architectural style

The drystone wall and the stone-tiled roof are the fundamental exterior elements of the Cotswold building tradition, defining the rude architectural dialect. The first man-made feature that visitors notice is the hundreds of miles of drystone walls (cumulatively longer than the Great Wall of China), following the ridges and dipping into the valleys of the hills, linking buildings into farmyards, encompassing and defining roads and country lanes, gardens, cattle pounds, field enclosures and sheep walks. The techniques of building walls in drystone, laid without mortar as it is dug from the fields, can be found already in carefully laid fragments of rubble stone on the horned entrance forecourts of Neolithic long barrows, such as Belas Knapp and Hetty Pegler's Tump at

Above: *Owlpen Manor, near Uley. Etching by F. L. Griggs, 1930, dedicated to his friend Norman Jewson, 'who saved this ancient house from ruin' in 1926.*

Left: *Abbotswood, near Stow-on-the-Wold. The Victorian garden front of 1866 seen obliquely (right), and Edwin Lutyens's new wing and the fountain court of 1901–02 to the left.*

Uley of the third millennium BC. The drystone wall evolved into the rubble wall, increasingly squared and coursed, then the mortared wall of sawn stone, with fine quality of finish in the dressings, especially in the bay windows and elegant doorways.

Sawn ashlar was cut at Querns in Cirencester for the Roman defences around the *oppidum*, which became a major provincial centre in the Roman Britain of the fourth century. About forty villa sites survive in an area known as a favoured resort of the Roman overlords, giving the Cotswolds the highest density of Roman villas in Britain. Sporadic survivors such as the opulent villa of Woodchester, whose mosaic pavement of Orpheus is one of the best north of the Alps, and the National Trust's Chedworth, laid out in a courtyard, with an apsidal temple of Mars, are the first recognisably Cotswold houses.

The Roman Fosse Way is the Cotswolds' most famous arterial route, much of it still in use today, running the length of the hills, linking settlements from Exeter to Lincoln. Apart from roads and tenacious street plans, there is no continuity through the 'Dark Ages'. By the end of the fourth century, nothing was left of the towns they served: Corinium, Roman Cirencester, at one time the second city in Roman Britain, faded away and expired in misery, to be colonised by Anglo-Saxon farmers. The site of a Saxon hall has been excavated in Tewkesbury, 120 feet long.

There are many early references to thatched roofs, even in the central Cotswolds. But the typical Cotswold roof – from, say, the fourteenth century – is laid in stone 'slates' to a steep pitch, averaging 52 degrees, used in nearly all the houses in this book. They appear already on the Roman villa at Chedworth. Equally, without discrimination they cap the humble cottages and hovels, barns, byres and shippons of the

the River Coln, with a mill mentioned in Domesday and the Elizabethan manor house of Bibury Court, led Alexander Pope to refer in 1726 to 'the pleasing prospect of Bibury' and William Morris to pronounce it 'surely the most beautiful village in England'.

Essentially the Cotswold style is a stone vernacular. There is a consonance of materials and technique whose functional qualities were tested and well understood over many generations. The vernacular tradition matured as an architectural language and rose to the challenge of the great domestic rebuilding of the early modern period, and in revivals, restorations or pastiches, it adapted, weakened or improved, but never vanished. It often survives best in the great houses and their dependencies. In high status buildings the expression of the tradition is at its most articulate, and modulates with inflexions, revivals and survivals according to fashion, as the craftsmanship of local masons adapts effortlessly from the Gothic of Beverston to the Classical

countryside; they were ubiquitous (at least until canals and railways brought Welsh slate to the edges of the hills), in stone 'presents' and 'pendles'. Traditionally, after quarrying, they were laid out on the fields for one winter to weather in the frost, and were hung by mutton-bone pegs, oak dowels, or copper – or today well-galvanised – nails. There are quaint local names, inconstant along the length of the hills, for the sizes of the slates, which diminish in gradations from the huge eaves course to ridge: cocks, wivots and cussoms, bachelors and long nines. They are carefully 'swept' with traditional 'galletting' along the valleys where the inclined planes meet.

There is a variety of size, shape, thickness and texture – no two tiles are ever exactly the same – so that the well-laid roof is truly one of the glories of the region. It should last at least two hundred years. The roof evolved with enrichments to gables and dormers, with stone details and mouldings to ridges, tablings and parapets. The refinement of the Cotswold style is the emphatic gable with a ridge nearly as high as the roof, sometimes nearly touching its neighbours either side at the plate. The high gable ends often have stone copings to protect the walls from ingress of damp. They can be seen in the famous cottages at Arlington Row, Bibury, where the low eaves are broken by a haphazard jumble of gables and dormers. This terrace of traditional cottages, grouped along

Top left: *Dodington Park, near Chipping Sodbury. Looking through the stately hall screen of 1810 to the Rococo staircase from Fonthill Splendens, a Palladian house built after 1756, demolished in 1808.*

Above: *Wormington Grange, near Broadway. The Neo-Greek east front by Henry Hakewill, 1826–28; the tetrastyle portico is based on the Temple of Ilissus, near Athens (demolished).*

Right: *Arlington Row, Bibury. Village picturesque dating to the late medieval period. Rack Isle is the water meadow to the right, where the weavers hung out their cloth to dry on racks.*

Renaissance of Stanway or Lodge Park, the Palladian proportions at Barrington or the Baroque exuberance at Barnsley Park, the carefully crafted Gothic Revival at Woodchester or picturesque Anglo-Indian at Sezincote, to return and recapitulate with vernacular revival in the Arts and Crafts manner at Rodmarton.

There are notable absences among Cotswold houses. There are no great courtier houses of the medieval period. No great castles or palaces. There are no iconic Palladian houses of the Whig aristocracy: even a political fortress like Cirencester House is Tory. There are no major houses by Soane, though he contributed to several. But there is a representative tier of dignified houses where many of the most famous English architects worked and prospered. They include William Kent at Badminton, possibly Barrington and Sherborne, the circle of Inigo Jones at Lodge Park and Stanway House, the Wyatt dynasty at Dodington Park, Lasborough and Newark, Robert Smirke at Cirencester Park, and William Talman at Dyrham.

The Cotswold house today

Today the Cotswold country house, with its farmhouses and cottages, can still lay claim to be the symbol of Englishness that it was for the early *Country Life* writers, and readers. But the houses have changed, adapting to the complex challenges of the second half of the twentieth century. It is a truism that they retain a disproportionate dominance in the landscape and local culture, forming the principal attractions of a successful tourist industry, which in rural areas has overtaken agriculture as the main local employer. They are no longer (principally) retreats, but reach out more broadly as they excel in their provision for public leisure, education and amenity. They provide the focus for the threatened traditions of fox hunting, as before, but are also exposed as venues for television dramas, polo matches at Cirencester, three-day-eventing at Badminton, trade fairs, battle re-enactments. New enterprises flourish, based on garden centres, highly successful farm shops, such as Daylesford, wedding venues, corporate events and holiday cottages, business units in adapted out-barns. There are seminars at Highgrove, education in heritage skills at Woodchester, which have extended the relevance even of smaller houses beyond the city and suburbs, to an international market place.

The Cotswolds are not just the visible country houses, of course. The built heritage of the region is now recognised as incomparable. In the Cotswold District Local Authority area alone there are more listed buildings of architectural or

historic interest and conservation areas than any area in Britain outside the City of Westminster: at least 6,400 listed structures. The Cotswolds have some of the best country churches, from the glorious wool churches of the Perpendicular at Northleach, Fairford and Cirencester to the simple Norman churches such as Duntisbourne Rous, on the wolds, and William Morris's favourite Inglesham in the Thames Valley. The Cotswolds and their houses are among the most successful tourism regions; the Area of Outstanding Natural Beauty, with 85,000 residents, is visited by 38 million day visitors every year.

Of course, the Cotswolds and its houses have not escaped painful change since the first issue of *Country Life* appeared in January 1897, at a time when agricultural rents were already declining. Few houses remain in the hands of the families that owned them when *Country Life* first described them. On the other hand, compared with other regions, remarkably few of the large Cotswold country houses were demolished in the disastrous post-war period, when they became unworkable as social systems. The list of the fallen includes: Fairford Park, demolished in 1957, one of the best; The Ridge had already been demolished in about 1934; Colesbourne Park (demolished in 1956–58; though a fragment remains, with a simplified new house on the site designed by Henry Elwes, the owner); Kingscote Park (demolished in 1951); Owlpen House (by S. S. Teulon, demolished in 1957); Ebworth House (burnt down as a fire training exercise in 1966); Estcourt Park (demolished in 1966); and Kiftsgate Court (substantially demolished in 1954). None of these was a house of sufficient architectural quality to have been recorded by *Country Life*.

Despite some creeping suburbanisation and unsympathetic expansion mostly on the fringes of villages and market towns, the appeal of the Cotswolds has survived undiminished into the twenty-first century. A new spirit of 'critical regionalism' has ensured that the subtle inflections of its craft traditions continue to be cherished, studied, and understood way beyond the region, as vital elements of an identity-giving culture. Quarries have closed, and stone has been replaced by new substitute materials, imported or manufactured – above all reconstituted stone and concrete blocks, and 'hard' surface textures. Improved communications have brought an uneasy nearness to London and the urban centres of the Midlands, destroying the remoteness by which the rural character of the Cotswolds endured into the twentieth century.

There is some optimism that a new scholarship in conservation and the craft techniques of lime repair, inspired by the Arts and Crafts movement, has continued the process of renewal that began in the late nineteenth century. Even recently, the National Trust has rescued old houses from an uncertain fate. Chastleton was described by John Julius Norwich in 1985 with the caveat: you'd better go there quick, or it might not be there to greet you. The royal patronage of the Prince of Wales and the Princess Royal, who have both established their country homes in the Cotswolds, has been an index of as well as a spur to the success of the region.

My own memory of the Cotswolds' many mansions is long, a time past that is eternally and urgently present. I have known most of the houses in this selection, and in many cases their owners – or increasingly parents and predecessors of owners – over a short lifetime, which has seen unprecedented change, not just visually to architecture and landscape. Agriculture has declined as the staple industry of the countryside, and the tie to the land has been finally broken, possibly for ever. The houses remain, but the way of life within them, the micro-economy that supported them, has changed with a fault-line of discontinuity in the new global system. The neighbouring cottages I can see from the windows of my own house, inhabited into my own time by a shepherd, a coffin maker, a plantsman and a vet, have been taken over by a judge, a journalist and an entrepreneur, connected by the virtual infrastructure of the internet.

I have seen many of these houses, even in my own family, adapt from being centres of farms and working estates – and therefore busy communities – to become all too often trophy houses owned by absentee fugitives from the city, affluent pensioners, international tourists, empty for much of the year. Some houses, such as Lodge Park at Sherborne and Chastleton, are heritage attractions open to a loyal and appreciative public. Some have been adapted as hotels – Tortworth, Upper and Lower Slaughter Manors, Bibury Court and recently Barnsley House – or as schools, like Hatherop, Westonbirt and Rendcomb. Others, like Woodchester and Newark, have emerged from being abandoned ruins to be carefully repaired, responding under quasi-public guardianship to the conditions and needs of the managed heritage. Many, like Lasborough Park, Ozleworth Park and Gatcombe in the south, and Adlestrop in the north, were until recently sad and neglected, sometimes institutionalised, all too little known or loved or visited, and are now redeemed gloriously to resume their function as family houses. A few, like Daylesford and Sezincote, were revived by City money a generation before, in the 1940s and 1950s. While others have been quite recently subdivided into flats and time-share apartments: Lord Burlington's Northwick Park, Sherborne House, Stout's Hill, Charlton Park (just outside our area) and Nether Swell Manor. It is remarkable that some have survived the onslaughts of the twentieth century almost unscathed, as traditional aristocratic or gentry hubs of landed estates, still owned by their historic families of centuries: Badminton, Cirencester, Stanway, Berkeley, Chavenage and Sudeley.

The Cotswold house, in its setting of villages and the wider landscape of its limestone hills and deep combes, are what *Country Life*'s archive here celebrates and, importantly, carries forward. Thanks are due to the interpretation by its editors and photographers of the formal monuments of its past, that the Cotswold house has for over a century been venerated as a touchstone of the 'House Beautiful', and its survival against all the odds seems secure. There has been little new building. But the houses in this book show that the old ones continue to adapt in ingenious ways, to survive and revive as they have always done. At the same time, they serve their purpose as viable dwelling places for their occupants – even if they live, as I do, as owls among ruins.

Left: *Daneway, near Sapperton. The ' high building' of c.1674 and (down the slope) the two late medieval gables of the south front.*

Below: *Lodge Park, Sherborne. The hunting lodge, before 1634, with the rusticated portico supporting the balustraded viewing platform.*

CASTLES OF THE COTSWOLDS

There are few feudal castles extant in the Cotswolds. The area was settled and peaceable from early times, though there was a feudal battle at Nibley Green, near Wotton-under-Edge, following a long drawn-out squabble over inheritances between William, Lord Berkeley, and Thomas Talbot, Viscount Lisle, as late as 1470, said to be the last, private, pitched battle in England. Domestic planning round court-yards, within moats and enclosing walls, and defensive features are as likely to be ornamental archaisms in chivalric taste as functional necessities.

There were the usual timber castles, moats, and fortified manor houses of which little or nothing remains. Brimpsfield, Newington Bagpath, Miserden and Upper Slaughter are post-Conquest mottes remaining as sometimes impressive unexcavated mounds of earth. The motte at Brimpsfield was succeeded by a stone castle, demolished by 1327. There is also some evidence of earthworks at Castle Godwyn, now known for its eighteenth-century house, described on page 97.

Above: *Entrance to the detached gatehouse built by Maurice de Gant, c.1229, at Beverston Castle.*

Left: *Berkeley Castle and terraces from the west: the shell keep to the left, dating from 1153, is the oldest part of Britain's oldest inhabited castle. The Berkeley family have lived here for 900 years. The inner gatehouse is to the right.*

Berkeley Castle, Gloucestershire

Berkeley Castle is the noblest of all, a marcher castle commanding the Vale of Severn. It stands proud on a stone ridge over the river meadows in an open-grained tufa stone with a mauve-grey tinge, by the percolation of iron, described tellingly as 'the colour of old brocade' in the old guide book by Vita Sackville-West. It is more than any other in this book a place of superlatives. It claims to be England's oldest continuously inhabited castle, the oldest domestic building still in use in the county of Gloucestershire, and is remarkable for being continuously inhabited by the same Berkeley (FitzHarding) family for 900 years. It dates from 1117; the feudal shell keep of 1153–56 still stands, revetting the earlier (1067) motte of the Norman magnate, William FitzOsbern.

Berkeley Castle lies just outside the hill region proper, but the baronial territory, or 'harness', of the Berkeleys dominated a huge tract of the south Cotswolds, along the hills from Tetbury to the outskirts of Bristol and Gloucester. Numerous manor houses were built within it for cadet branches, relations, or sometimes henchmen and dependants, of the Berkeley overlords, of which not a few survive today, including Bradley Court, Dodington, Wanswell Court, Stoke Park, Little Sodbury, and Yate Court.

The Berkeleys held several castles in the area, including one at Dursley, which the antiquary John Leland, visiting in 1540, described as, 'fell to decay and is clean taken down', and at Wotton-under-Edge. The latter was in truth a fortified courtier house, dismantled for its building materials in time for a visit

Above: *The feudal castle, a rugged agglomeration in mauve-grey stone, viewed over the level meadows from the south; in medieval times, these could be flooded at will for defence.*

Right: *The inner bailey. The hexagonal entrance tower (centre) leads to the great hall (left) and state rooms (right). The French Gothic doorway was inserted as part of thoroughgoing improvements in the 1920s, following the sale of Berkeley Square in London.*

by Henry VII to Berkeley Castle in 1491, and already a ruin by the date of Leland's visit.

Thomas, 8th Lord Berkeley, was the great builder of the family, building in the court Decorated style of the fourteenth century. To him we can attribute the building of Thorpe Tower and the extensive domestic range at Berkeley Castle, begun in 1326, adapting the feudal power base as a palatial residence in more settled times. The great hall, where the last jester in England fell to his death from the minstrels' gallery as late as 1728, has a fine timber roof, screens from a Berkeley estate in Glamorganshire and the distinctive 'Berkeley' polygonal arches. It is flanked at the upper end by the state rooms (now two drawing rooms) and chapel (now the morning room), which has the translations from the Book of Revelations (1387) of John Trevisa, a castle chaplain, written faintly on the beams; and at the lower end by the octagonal kitchen and service rooms (shown as a dining room today).

The Berkeley family were alienated from their estates in the sixteenth century. There were some improvements to the castle in the early seventeenth century (such as the main staircase of 1637) and the keep was slighted in the Civil War. The castle acquired impressive Baroque gardens on the south-facing terraces illustrated in engravings by Kip, Buck and Marklove. But generally there were few alterations in the seventeenth, eighteenth and nineteenth centuries, showing remarkable conservatism and restraint, when the Berkeleys reigned undisputed as the grandest Whig family in Gloucestershire. They were content to continue doggedly in their feudal and increasingly unfashionable fortress, tinkering and making small improvements to the living accommodation, but nothing more.

In 1874, there were repairs – notably to the hall – under Philip Webb, the leading Arts and Crafts architect (who worked at Forthampton Court near Tewkesbury), but there was none of the usual drastic Neo-Gothic restoration of the Victorian period. The castle's drastic modernisation came in due course in the 1920s, when, following the sale of Berkeley Square in London, it was improved by the 8th and last Earl Berkeley with imported fragments (the hall fireplace and screens) from elsewhere on the Berkeley estates and notably with French Gothic architectural antiques, remodelling the state rooms. The Berkeleys of Spetchley in Worcestershire, distant collaterals, inherited in 1942, and continue gallantly today, lineal descendants after 900 years, wrestling with roofs and hunting the hounds. Berkeley and its family seem eternal.

The castle from the west with its Victorian overgrowth of ivy and topiary yews – now vanished – on the sheltered lower terrace.

Beverston Castle, Gloucestershire

Beverston, near Tetbury, was also a Berkeley seat, and is the only Cotswold castle still standing. Although 'many ages more ancient than Berkeley', the best of what remains is relatively late, a fragment dating from the time of Thomas, 8th Lord Berkeley, in the fourteenth century.

Beverston's history is as old as England itself. Earl Godwin held it as his headquarters with his sons in 1051, and set forth from here to do battle with Edward the Confessor. King Stephen and the Empress Matilda joined in combat here before 1140. It was rebuilt and 'turreted' by Maurice de Gant, 'without the king's licence', shortly before he was given a permission to crenellate in 1229. Two round towers still stand from his small quadrangular bastion, with part of a picturesque twin-towered gatehouse.

In 1330, Thomas Berkeley purchased the manor, and over the following six years, according to John Smyth, 'much repaired and beautified [the castle], with the park adjoining … where he spent many months in the year'. He was lord of Berkeley Castle at the time of the grisly murder of Edward II just three years before (in 1327). He upgraded the comforts of the early defensive building as a fortified manor house for residential use, adding his Berkeley Tower – impressive work, built (according to Smyth) at the time of the Black Death, in 1348–49. The west range of Thomas's castle still stands more or less intact, containing a solar above a vaulted undercroft, and flanked at the angles with square towers.

An ingenious stair contrived within the walls ascends to Thomas's private rooms. A first-floor chapel, with access to the solar and hall, is of the courtly standard we associate with him at Berkeley, with the best Gothic detailing of any house in the

Right: *The unrestored east gatehouse with a guardroom entrance and grooves for the portcullis.*

Below: *The castle block stands forlornly across the moat to the left, dating to a rebuild by Thomas Lord Berkeley in the 1340s. The present domestic wing, to the right, was probably added after a fire in 1691, on the site of the medieval hall.*

Cotswolds: vaulted ceilings, rich double sedilia with crocketed heads, and a *piscina*. Above the chapel there is another private oratory giving off Lord Berkeley's chamber, which had a circular window taking up virtually the whole west wall. The two-storey gatehouse to the east was probably added by him, of which one tower is extant. It has the usual guardrooms with lodging over, grooves for an immense portcullis in the archway, and a drawbridge over the moat.

Thomas Berkeley ran huge flocks of sheep here, consolidating sheep walks, and shearing as many as 5,775 sheep in 1333 in his manors round Beverston, where one year he stocked the demesne land with 1500 wethers. This was the summit of Beverston's short-lived prosperity, when it was a township with its own fair and market.

The descendants of one of Thomas's younger sons, calling themselves the Berkeleys of Beverstone, sold in 1597 to Sir John Poyntz. By 1612, Beverston was in the hands of Sir Michael Hicks-Beach, of the same family as Sir Baptist Hicks, the great benefactor of Chipping Campden and ancestor of the Earls St Aldwyn. In the Civil War, the castle was besieged, defeated by stealth following the capture of the Royalist commander, Colonel Oglethorpe, and slighted by Colonel Massey, whose headquarters were at Chavenage, next door. The castle has never recovered. Following a fire in 1691, the present house, a long block with mullioned and transomed windows, was built on the site of the medieval south range, retaining the west wall. Inside there is a fine staircase with oak balusters.

The Hicks-Beaches sold in 1842, when the estate was added to the Holford family's extensive landholdings centred on Westonbirt. The castle had already declined to a farmhouse and a model village was built to the order of the Holfords, with cottages lining the road which were probably designed by Lewis Vulliamy in simplified Tudor, with distinctive bargeboards and Gothic porches.

The castle lives on as a ruinous hulk of towers and ivy-mantled walls, pitted by time, impenetrable beyond the road and a dry moat, with a medieval barn and church forming the backdrop to a romantic garden. It was created by Mrs Arthur Strutt after she bought the estate as war broke out in 1939, and was illustrated following her improvements in *Country Life* in 1944. It remains, for all the romance of its history, little known.

Above: *A large hearth in the 1691 wing, rebuilt for the Hicks-Beach family on the scale of a comfortable manor house.*

Right: *The late-seventeenth-century staircase to the south range, with widely-set oak balusters.*

Sudeley Castle, Gloucestershire

Sudeley Castle, Winchcombe, is set splendidly in a wide and wooded combe under the Cotswold escarpment. It is not a castle in the sense of a feudal fastness, fortified and defensive, or an instrument of conquest. As it stands it is a late Tudor courtier's house, which has swollen into a royal palace, rambling round two courtyards like an Oxbridge college. It has two queens to boast of, and acquired plenty of royal connections. As it achieved the glory of royal ownership and occupation, Elizabethan and Stuart remodelling and aggrandisement inevitably followed.

Sudeley preserves its gaunt skyline of defensive towers and battlements, which can never have been very effective for military purposes, and failed when they were put to the test in the Civil War. Then it was slighted and all but abandoned for two centuries, when it declined to a romantic ruin. Its nineteenth-century thoroughgoing restoration by the Dent brothers, magnate glovers from Worcestershire, translated it into a comfortable Victorian country house.

Its recorded history is as long as that of any house in the Cotswolds. It first occurs as a manor of Ethelred the Unready, who gave it to his daughter Goda, sister of Edward the Confessor. The Sudeleys of Sudeley (and then the Tracys of Toddington) were heirs, claiming direct descent from Charlemagne, and were settled here before the Conquest.

The castle and manor came into the possession of the Boteler family of Wem, Shropshire, by marriage after the Black Death, when the history of the present castle begins. It was mainly built by Ralph Boteler after 1442, when he was appointed Lord High Admiral of England, and it preserves his plan of two courtyards, set at a canted angle – the whole *enceinte* was probably originally moated. Only the gatehouse and two towers at the angles of the inner court remain.

During the Wars of the Roses the Botelers backed the wrong side, and Sudeley was forfeited to the Crown, whose property it remained from 1469 to 1547. The Tudor kings granted it as a prize to a succession of loyal courtiers and favourites. Edward IV first granted it to his brother, Richard 'Crouchback', Duke of Gloucester. He upgraded the accommodation to a royal standard in the 1470s, with new apartments of state (largely in ruins today).

There followed the Dukes of Buckingham and Bedford. Henry VIII visited on a progress with Anne Boleyn in 1535, a year before she was tried and beheaded. Late in his reign, it became the seat of his Queen, Katherine Parr, the last of his six wives, who alone survived him, and who had secured the house from her brother, William Parr, Marquis of Northampton. Henry VIII died in 1547, and his successor, the boy-king Edward VI, gave Sudeley to his favourite uncle by marriage, Sir Thomas Seymour, who was created Baron Sudeley (and Lord High Admiral of England).

Sudeley had a fraught afterlife as the dashing Prince Rupert's base during the Civil War, strategically placed between the Royalist headquarters in Oxford and supporters in the West. It was besieged and sacked by Colonel Edward Massey, who laid waste to so many other Cotswold houses. He removed the roofs and his men plundered the chapel and desecrated the graves, including that of Queen Katherine Parr.

Two centuries of decline followed. Katherine's grave was rediscovered in 1782, when the increasingly picturesque ruin became a shrine. A fine series of John Buckler watercolours

Top: *Sudeley Castle and the double yew hedge (planted in 1856) from the south, showing the ivy-mantled, long east range, and chapel (right) restored by Sir George Gilbert Scott.*

Above: *The west end of the chapel of c.1460, with its corbelled bell turret. Queen Katherine Parr was buried here in 1548.*

document its state of abandonment in 1818. They had been commissioned by the Duke of Buckingham and Chandos, who had bought Sudeley Castle from Lord Rivers of Stratfield Saye, in 1810, with the intention of restoring it. Sir John Soane drew up plans, but they were never carried out, as they were too expensive. The habitable part of the castle declined to a wayfarers' inn, known as the Castle Arms, as the building reached the nadir of its long history.

Its modern history begins after two bachelor brothers, William and John Dent, acquired first the estate from Lord Rivers in 1830 and then the castle from the Duke of Buckingham in 1837. Men of antiquarian sympathies, they commissioned Harvey Eginton of Worcester to rebuild the castle (1837–40) in the spirit of the Romantic Revival, distinctly, flamboyantly *faux*. He made the outer court ready for the brothers' habitation, and improved the picturesque ruins of the inner court, reinstating features such as 'correct' fan vaulting and hood moulds. The Dents began to acquire Tudor objects to furnish the house, notably at the Strawberry Hill sale in 1842, the nucleus of its superb collections.

William Dent died in 1854 and on John's death in 1855, the estate passed to their nephew, John Coucher Dent, who had married Emma Brocklehurst, an heiress, in 1847. They continued to oversee a thoroughgoing redecoration and restoration (1854–57) of the castle and chapel under Sir George Gilbert Scott – or, more accurately, his pupil, John Drayton Wyatt. His hand lies heavily on Sudeley. The inside of the chapel was rebuilt (virtually), except for the sedilia, despite Ruskin's (and by then Emma Dent's) protestations. It is redeemed by good detailing and quality in glass and pews and fittings, and contains the tomb of Queen Katherine Parr, in which her remains were reinterred in 1861. Drayton Wyatt is also responsible for the gatehouse and the Neo-Gothic north tower building in the outer court, dated 1886–90.

Emma Dent reigned for nearly half a century as Sudeley's energetic and imaginative Victorian châtelaine. A cultivated

Above: *The long panelled library, with its Elizabethan fireplace of Edmund Chandos, was remodelled by Walter Godfrey in 1930.*

Right: *A corner of Queen Katherine Parr's room, with the Neo-Tudor ceiling, Swiss and German glass inserted in the oriel window, and a collection of portrait miniatures.*

collector, and much-loved philanthropist of the town of Winchcombe, she filled the house with good things, buying pictures, literary manuscripts, collecting relics and memorabilia of Katherine Parr and Charles I. Early photographs in *Country Life* show how studiously she developed the antiquarian mood her uncles-in-law had created, with rampant ivy softening the façades, replanting the gardens with formal parterres and yews, and expansive lawns. Emma died childless in 1900, when her nephew inherited, hyphenating his name as Henry Dent-Brocklehurst.

The plan of two courtyards is preserved from the time of Boteler, though they are joined awkwardly now where the cross-range has been destroyed. The outer court, apart from the old north gateway, is late Elizabethan; the lodgings are of about 1577, with some fine Renaissance-Classical detail to the fenestration in the textbook style of Kirby House, Northamptonshire. It leads to the older inner court, retaining the original range of the 1440s to the west. The south range where the hall would have stood is sadly missing; the west range probably comprised the royal apartments of Richard 'Crouchback', still standing a full two-storey high, but defiantly in ruins, with fireplaces stranded at first-floor level, as if left by an outgoing tide.

In the habitable part of the castle, the interiors, 'scraped' and panelled or relined, have lost their ancient patina, and some highlights from the collections have been dispersed (including paintings by Constable and Poussin). Improvements were made in the 1930s by Walter Godfrey, who raised floor levels, inserted panelling, new bay windows and radically moved Tudor fireplaces around. In the 1980s, the John Fowler firm adapted the old kitchens and servants' hall in the private apartments.

Mark Dent-Brocklehurst inherited in 1949, and began to open the house and garden to the public as one of the Cotswolds' most popular attractions. His widow, Elizabeth, now Lady Ashcombe, continues the inspired traditions of Emma Dent as the driving force behind the development of the glorious gardens and new exhibitions, as the castle provides a home for three families.

The east range with the library bays added by Walter Godfrey and the terminal north-east tower completed by John Drayton Wyatt in 1890.

THE COTSWOLD MANOR HOUSE

The Cotswolds are epitomised by their manorial architecture and groupings, and their Tudor and early Stuart manor houses were celebrated from early days by *Country Life* as symbols of the enduring values of English civilisation. Edward Hudson and H. Avray Tipping inspired a group of gentlemen-owners to buy and repair a number of important early manor houses in or near the Cotswolds: Avebury and Westwood Manor in Wiltshire; Cold Ashton and Hazelbury Manor in Gloucestershire; and Lytes Cary and Cothay in Somerset. The Arts and Crafts architects who settled in the area in the late nineteenth century were the driving force behind the adaptation and repair of many more: Kelmscott, Daneway, Owlpen, Burford Priory.

All these early houses are complex hybrids, often only partly medieval, now with more circumspection described as 'sub-medieval'. There are few medieval manor houses still intact in the Cotswolds, and those that remain are incomplete,

Above: *Bradley Court, Wotton-under-Edge. The south front, almost symmetrical with twin staircase towers and central porch, has been little altered since it was built for a cadet branch of the Berkeley family in 1559.*

Left: *Daneway, near Sapperton. The main south front. The high building of c.1674 stands to the right. The rusticated doorway in the centre leads to an inner courtyard; to the left, are twin gables fronting the medieval core. The sundial above the doorway is dated 1717.*

fragments incorporated into later houses, or were radically altered in the 'great rebuilding' of the sixteenth and seventeenth centuries. Many of these are conservative in style, retaining the standard medieval arrangement of planning – with a hall in the centre entered at the 'lower' end, flanked by service rooms and the family parlour/solar block at the 'upper' end – if with an increasing symmetry to the main façades. Good examples of medieval houses lie just outside the Cotswold region. Great Chalfield in Wiltshire is a textbook manorial group of the fifteenth century, all in stone, whose restoration by Sir Harold Brakspear was so admired by Tipping in *Country Life* in 1914.

The following houses are good examples of these early Cotswold manors. Iron Acton Court, in the Severn Vale, was taken over in 1986 by English Heritage, having survived untouched by the Victorian and Edwardian generations as a romantic and fragmentary ruin in rose-pink Pennant stone. Careful excavation and analysis has since uncovered its long evolution through the medieval period, retaining a courtyard plan. It was the seat of Nicholas Poyntz, whose family had settled there in 1364. He rebuilt the medieval house, probably thirteenth century in origin, and in a matter of months added a new block hastily prepared for the entertainment of Henry VIII and Anne Boleyn in 1535, fitted out in the latest fashion, with wall paintings at frieze level in 'antike' work.

A range at Horton Court, near Chipping Sodbury, includes a freestanding (and uninhabited) Norman hall of about 1150, with two matching doorways, enriched, and some round-arched windows. It is one of the oldest halls in England and was probably built for Robert de Beaufeu, Rector of Horton and Prebendary of Salisbury Cathedral, or his successor.

Southrop Manor, near Lechlade, is also an early manor house with Norman survivals, though it appears a conventional mid-seventeenth-century house today. Fragments shows its greater antiquity, notably a tower structure by the church, which is all that remains of the original Norman manor house. A late Norman doorway, moved by Norman Jewson in 1926, forms the entrance to the present dining room.

The Cotswolds are overwhelmingly a country of fine market towns, with plenty of good buildings and entire streets reared on the profits of wool. Burford and Bourton-on-the-Water are popular tourist honey pots, well manicured, overflowing with tearooms and antique shops. Tetbury, Stow-on-the-Wold, Minchinhampton, Lechlade and Painswick are centres famous for their picturesque groups of traditional buildings. Northleach, Winchcombe, Fairford and Cirencester have outstanding wool churches of the late Perpendicular. Cirencester, known as 'Ci'ceter' into my youth, was one of the

Top: *Iron Acton Court, Severn Vale. The east range of the Tudor courtier house in Pennant stone, largely rebuilt by Sir Nicholas Poyntz after 1534, seen through the Renaissance gateway from the road.*

Above: *Down Ampney House, near Cirencester. The loss of this twin-towered gatehouse of 1537 following a fire in 1963 was a tragedy.*

Right: *Burford Priory, Burford. The late-seventeenth-century long gallery (left) and the chapel (right) with its unusual rose window in Gothic Revival style added about 1662.*

main wool markets, and is the nearest to a regional capital.

Chipping Campden is architecturally perhaps the most distinguished of them all, with several good early houses. Its merchant houses, though in a country town, are at the root of the pedigree of the smaller country house in the Cotswolds. The most famous of them is Grevel House, reputedly built about 1380 for William Grevel (d.1401), 'the flower of the wool merchants of all England'. With its fine doorway and Perpendicular oriel window of two storeys facing onto the street, cusped windows, and panelled tracery and gargoyles at the angles above, it already marks the emergence of a recognisably 'Cotswold' style.

Woolstaplers' Hall built for Robert Calf is almost opposite, possibly the solar range of what was a grander merchant house, late fourteenth century in origin. It was the home of the great Arts and Crafts designer, C. R. Ashbee, from 1902 to 1911, who restored it, exposing wonderful Gothic detailing and an oriel window with tracery in a first-floor room, and incorporating an early timber-framed barn into the house.

All the houses in Broadway are said to be built and roofed in the stone from the quarries at the top of Broadway Hill. The eastern part of Court Farm incorporates part of the hall of a cruck-framed house of the late fourteenth century. The so-called 'Tudor House' corresponded to the ideal of the Cotswold house cultivated by the early *Country Life*, a picturesque four-storey building with triple gables to the street. The centre of the street elevation is emphasised by a bay window to the ground and first floors, on the parapet of which are two shields bearing the dates 1659 and 1660.

Abbot's Grange is another distinguished early Broadway house celebrated by *Country Life*. When this 'gateway' town was the resort of artists at the turn of the twentieth century, it became the property and studio of F. D. Millet. It is a hall house of fourteenth century origins, with an oratory projecting at the south east and a solar with its undercroft at the southern end.

The church and in particular the religious orders controlled huge tracts of land in the Cotswolds in the Middle Ages, and became significant stakeholders in the fortunes of the wool trade. This is apparently the origin of the local saying: 'As sure as God's in Gloucestershire'. Many of the early country houses have a monastic history or connection as summer retreats for the medieval abbots, outlying priories or granges, or rented properties, sometimes with notable tithe barns in Cotswold stone. Stanway, for example, was for centuries a country house of the Abbots of Tewkesbury. Many later country houses were rebuilt out of the ruins of the monasteries after the Dissolution. Chavenage House was allegedly built out of the stones of Horsley Priory, Newark Park out of those of Kingswood Abbey. While Cirencester House is said to stand on the site of the castle, Richard Master built a Jacobean house over the cloisters of the medieval Abbey.

H. Avray Tipping described the salvation of Burford Priory, just in Oxfordshire, in the early years of the twentieth century as 'a brand saved from the burning.' It was regarded by his generation as one of the most important Tudor houses in the Cotswolds, and was one of the first to be described in *Country Life* in 1911. The house was all but demolished and abandoned in the early nineteenth century, and altered drastically after 1808 at a time when the fate of so many early Cotswold houses hung in the balance. Colonel La Terrière undertook the early-twentieth-century restoration, and, as Tipping commented with approval, 'combined a love of old architecture with practical knowledge and sound methods of dealing with quite decayed examples of it.' He published the photographs taken in 1908, before the intervention of La Terrière, comparing it with the pictures afterwards, when he lavished characteristic praise on 'the preservation of the surface; every old feature has been retained and the aspect of venerable age preserved.' The repair work was massive, and was continued after 1911 by his successor, the tea trader, MP and collector E. J. Horniman, under Walter Godfrey, the antiquarian architect of Lewes. What stands today is (mostly) a confident restoration for these two patrons.

The original house was an Augustinian hospital dedicated to St John the Evangelist. The Elizabethan owner was Sir Lawrence Tanfield, a lawyer, who built the main range of the E-shaped house and entertained James I here in 1603. William Lenthall, Speaker of the Long Parliament, acquired it from his successors in 1634, adding on the chapel and other features. Charles II dined here in 1681. The long, late seventeenth-

century range was rebuilt, the interiors retaining excellent early fireplaces, doors and twisted columns, with a ceiling to the great chamber of 1662. The chapel of the same date is early Gothic Revival rather than Survival, with some astonishing virtuoso mason's work of the period, including a relief of Moses and the burning bush, supported by flanking angels standing on stocky columns.

Prinknash Park (now St Peter's Grange) was, like Frocester Court in the Vale, a summer house of the Abbots of Gloucester, and its core is by definition a pre-Reformation house. After losing Prinknash at the Dissolution, Benedictine monks came back from Caldey Island in 1928, when they received the house under the will of Thomas Dyer Edwardes, who had advertised it for sale in *Country Life* in 1923.

Medieval fabric remains, and there are gables, an oriel, and the arms of Katherine of Aragon of the sixteenth century. The main building, including the central range, was executed for Abbot William Parker, about 1521–25, to an H-plan. The porch was probably added by Sir John Bridgeman, who bought the manor and park in 1628 with his son George, following his removal from Owlpen. The chapel was dedicated in 1629, and the house was used as a Royalist base during the siege of Gloucester.

The house has been badly altered by good architects, including Ewan Christian, F. W. Waller, Harold Brakspear, J. Coats-Carter and Harry Goodhart-Rendell, a generous benefactor to the community, whose design for the new abbey was alas never executed. At the time of writing, the monks, having built a new abbey in 1968–72, are planning to move back into 'St Peter's Grange'.

If Prinknash is the last of the pre-Reformation, Horton Court, already noted for its Norman hall described on page 34, is the first of the Renaissance, almost contemporary with Abbot Parker's work at Prinknash. The house has some of the earliest Classical detail in the country (*c.*1521), associated with courtier owners familiar with advanced developments on the Continent. The lintel of the doorcase has an entablature decorated with bold *paterae* and jambs with strapwork in confident Mannerist arabesques and triumphs. There is also a chapel and a wonderful six-bay Renaissance loggia, free-standing by the tulip tree in the garden.

The loggia contains a row of moulded busts, plaques in low relief set into the back wall, suggesting Antiquity. At first sight they seem to be crude and conventional Imperial medallions, a galumphing version of a portrait bronze by Pisanello, perhaps. But a scheme of humanist iconography has been identified, showing that the carefully chosen heroes and anti-heroes depicted, alternately Roman and provincial, are a learned commentary on the ups and downs of the career of a diplomat. For the builder, William Knight, was a clerk in the King's service, educated (partly) in Rome, and an emissary of Henry VIII to the Pope, charged with vain negotiations over the Royal divorce. The detail could date from before Knight's spell in Rome and derive from Low Country sources, already widely available. In 1550, Horton was granted by the Crown to the recusant Paston family of Norfolk, who set up a chapel in the attics when they finally moved here in 1707. The interiors were restored for the Dudley Wards in 1927 to 1932, when they were written up in *Country Life*. The house was presented to the National Trust in 1946.

Down Ampney House, near Cirencester, was probably built for the courtier Sir Edmund Hungerford after his retirement in 1470; the open hall is of that date, in four bays with carved queen-post trusses. Soane altered the house for Sir John Eliot in 1799, with Gothic details answering the old fabric for once with an antiquarian respect. *Country Life* serves as a paper of record here, for tragically the twin-towered gatehouse of 1537 was demolished following a fire in 1963. The composer Ralph Vaughan-Williams was born in the village.

It is now possible to date Bradley Court, near Wotton-under-Edge, with some confidence to 1559, by the date stone above the entrance porch. In the thirteenth century it belonged to Hugo de Bradleia, but was bought by the 1st Lord Berkeley and remained a house of a cadet branch of the great local family until 1611.

The house stands under Westridge Hill, with a rendered symmetrical front, set back from the lane. The porch is in the centre of a long, gabled façade, with two flanking stair towers, octagonal in plan; only the hall chimney-stack stands off-centre. It has been hardly touched externally since Kip's engraving of 1710, frozen in time, made when Thomas Dawes was owner. It was held by his successors, ultimately as a secondary house, into modern times. The house retains its medieval plan, with service rooms (off the lower end of the hall), and hall and parlour (now the library). A beautifully proportioned drawing room was added like a box at the rear (north) with the best bedroom over, attributed to Anthony Keck for its mouldings in stiff acanthus leaves and characteristic mahogany doors, c.1790.

Thomas and Penelope Messel, the present owners, have achieved a miraculous transformation, demolishing a clutter of nineteenth-century extensions at the rear, and furnishing the house with gilded creations of Thomas Messel's own design and early oak, which survived the fire at his family's house at Nymans in Sussex. The poet Seamus Heaney was a frequent visitor, describing the landscape 'Of topiary, lawn and brick | Possessed, interspaced, walled, nostalgic.'

Dixton Manor is dated 1555, a fragment of a much larger house recorded in the painting now in the Cheltenham Museum. Only the porch of that date survives, the rest is a rebuild, when a west wing was added at a right angle in the early Jacobean period.

Lypiatt Park, Bisley, is a composite house: in part genuine medieval, in part Elizabethan, and in part a nineteenth-century essay in Neo-Tudor, with some grand rebuilding by the Wyatts. Jeffry Wyatville, architect of the Neo-feudal work at Windsor Castle for George III, remodelled Lypiatt in a castellated Gothic Revival style in 1809–15, dramatically restyling the hall range and adding a new wing for the clothier owner, Paul Wathen. Wyatville's distant relation T. H. Wyatt took this further in 1876–77 in a more 'correct' Gothic style. The *Country Life* description of December 1900 says nothing to disillusion the reader that all the Wyatt family alterations are anything but genuine medieval work.

The north front is the main range of the Elizabethan manor house. The outbuildings of a large medieval manor house of the Maunsell family add a frame of authentic picturesque interest. The detached thirteenth-century granary is in splendid condition, with plate tracery to the north window, and a grain chute in the form of an ox's head. There is also a round dovecote of about the same date, and a late fourteenth-century Decorated chapel with nave and chancel, and a bellcote with two bells.

After being the country seat inherited by my uncle's amiable uncle, Judge Harry Woodcock and his sister Isla, exceptionally the house today is furnished not with the historical collections of the Cotswold country house; rather it contains in its whitewashed interiors arrangements of the sculpture of its celebrated post-war owner, Lynn Chadwick, who bought the house as demolition threatened in 1952, and established a Modernist interest in the house and gardens.

Top left: *Prinknash Park, near Gloucester. A summer house of the medieval Abbots of Gloucester with Tudor and Jacobean additions, it was heavily Victorianised in Tudor style.*

Above: *Lypiatt Park, Bisley. This (basically) early-sixteenth-century manor house was drastically restored by Jeffry Wyatville in Perpendicular Revival, with battlements and bays, and then by T. H. Wyatt in a more 'correct' Victorian Gothic.*

Top right: *Horton Court, near Chipping Sodbury. The open loggia, an ambulatory of six bays, was built for William Knight, diplomat and traveller, in the 1520s. It marks the germ of Continental Renaissance decoration in the Cotswolds.*

Daneway House, Gloucestershire

Daneway, one of the most romantically evocative as well as the oldest manor houses in the Cotswolds, is buried deep among woods. H. Avray Tipping in *Country Life* emphasised its solitude and changelessness, having 'kept modernity at a distance'. The place name apparently means 'road through the valley', and so it lies hidden down a narrow lane on rising ground beyond the estate village of Sapperton, though it is an outlying hamlet of Bisley parish. It is a size smaller than most, scarcely more than a farmhouse, where an accretion of modest stone roofs and gables is set off by a later tower wing to the south east – its only attempt at a note of grandeur.

The feeling is medieval, timeless, with a nucleus of early buildings with stone buttresses and tiny lancet or Perpendicular windows, but then a Classical doorway with a rusticated head appears rather incongruously in the centre of the main front. This garden front is organic, with a 'satisfying balance', noted Tipping, but without any pretence at symmetry. All is harmoniously coherent. Hussey judged it in *Country Life* (December 1934) a composition of sheer romance that is 'instinctively right'.

The main entrance is to the left (west). Inside, there are plenty of up-and-down steps, worn by numberless footfalls, as you walk from room to room vainly piecing together a complex structure of evolution, with floor levels cut into a slope. Gothic arches over doorways contrast in various styles, an ogive-headed doorway to the west, and, slightly later, a trefoil-arched one. A screens' passage transects the house from the front porch to a garden up some steps behind. Beyond the screens' passage to the west is a domestic cross-wing, with the contemporary undercroft, later altered as the kitchen, and a private apartment, or solar, above.

Left: *Steps to the buttressed service wing, with clipped box.*

Below: *The kitchen wing was probably added in the sixteenth century.*

The hall entered by its original stone archway is the kernel of the house, which has grown organically either side of it. At its eastern or 'high' end, it is dug inconveniently into the hillside. Its soot-blackened roof timbers are exposed in the room above, dating to the time when it was open to the roof, but it is now horizontally divided with an inserted floor. They have been securely dated by dendrochronology to about 1315.

The records at this date are sparse, but Henry Clifford and his wife Maud received a licence to build their oratory in 1340, probably sited above the south porch; licence to crenellate and hold Mass was given about 1380 to John Clifford, and the manor, described as a messuage and a plough-land, was held by him at his death in 1397. Daneway was sold in 1647 to William Hancox, whose family had already been lessees since 1532. By the time of the Civil War, William Hancox, who served as a captain in the Parliamentary forces, was High Constable of Bisley Hundred, and Hancoxes were treating with the Protector Cromwell himself. It was owned or occupied for over three centuries (until 1862) by this yeoman family.

The medieval hall house is still embedded in their later additions, though they modified and extended Daneway over the generations, marking the family's rise in the world. This was symbolised most notably with the addition of the so-called 'high building', a cross-gabled tower of five storeys, added shortly after inheriting the estate by William Hancox II (c.1674). The high building is set slightly askew to the main house, and there are steps from the courtyard outside leading up to a west entrance with a mannered doorway. There is one room per floor, accessed by a spiral stair in the north-west corner. The rooms have ribbed plasterwork ceilings and modelled details, such as a trout in the eponymous Trout Room. The high building was the last structure to be built, and nothing has been drastically altered since.

Above: *The early-fourteenth-century hall as used by Ernest Gimson to display his furniture, about 1911. The ceiling was inserted in the sixteenth century.*

Right: *The passage cuts through the core of the medieval house to the hall, with arches over the early doorways of various dates, and steps to the garden beyond. The trefoil-arched doorway to the left probably led to the oratory of about 1340.*

In the twentieth century, Daneway attracted a 'tribe' (as Morris's architect Philip Webb called them) of uncommonly creative and talented occupants. After being acquired in a state 'rather shabby, derelict and forlorn' by Lord Bathurst, it was restored by Ernest Barnsley in 1896, and let to Ernest Gimson from 1902 to 1919. He did not live at Daneway, but used the outbuildings for the manufacture, and the house for the display, of his remarkably innovative furniture. As such, the house was a legend for architect-designers of the Arts and Crafts movement.

Oliver Hill (1887–1968), architect, garden designer, architectural historian and contributor to *Country Life*, took on the house, with his wife Titania, from 1948. It was lovingly romanticised with Hill's heterodox clutter of textiles and antiques, and nurtured the formative years of his great-nephew, the sculptor Simon Verity, whose youthful blessing is graven on a buttress.

In 1994, Daneway was acquired by Nicholas and Kai Spencer, who became the first owner-occupiers for nearly a century. Wisely, they commissioned the best advice before intervening. The architect Nicholas Johnston planned a thoroughgoing but sensitive adaptation of the house. The Spencers reordered and extended the garden with formal yews and a new approach. There is a new lease of life, marked by fresh limewash throughout. Rory Young cut in slate the names of the craftsmen engaged in the repair work, in the Arts and Crafts tradition. On the small estate of about 300 acres, you will find Emily Young's sculpture of a shepherd striding the fields, thousands of young trees, and miles of new drystone walls. This magical house in its renewal remains a haven intact, enfolded in harmony with its landscape.

Left: *The high building is the latest work, a self-contained bachelor wing of c.1674, here viewed from the garden to the east.*

Below: *The enclosed terrace above the house was laid out by the present owners.*

Chavenage House, Gloucestershire

Chavenage is set quietly among lanes on the Cotswold uplands near Tetbury. It has evident charm, one of the early manor houses celebrated in *Country Life* by H. Avray Tipping as an ideal which 'exhibits a variety of styles, the handiwork of succeeding generations of owners.' An avenue of chestnut trees leads to a gateway to the west of the road, marking a short drive past sloping lawns and umbrageous cedars. It is aligned on the central porch, bearing in the diamond stops of the label the date 1576 and the initials 'ES' and 'IS', for Edward Stephens and Joan his wife, marking the ownership and rebuilding by a wool man who had bought the estate in 1564.

The core of the main house is convincingly medieval, but there are caveats, with signs of significant later phases of rebuilding. The porch has a Decorated, two-light window with tracery, but it is nowhere to be seen on an engraving of 1807, though it is said to have been reused from the dissolved Augustinian priory nearby at Horsley, or from the earlier manor house standing on the site.

The east entrance front is arranged in a standard E-plan, but asymmetrical; Tipping commented approvingly on the odd windows, eccentrically placed and of different shapes and sizes. The great hall has two striking windows, divided by a buttress, with gabled cross-wings at either side projecting forwards. The service wing is to the right (north) of the hall and the parlour wing to the left.

You enter the screens' passage by the early porch; the great hall within is spacious, of full storey height, with the double-

Above: *Elizabethan splendour. But the large bay window of the ballroom to the south front is Edwardian, and the church is an early-nineteenth-century hotch-potch made up of fragments.*

Right: *The oak room has sixteenth-century carvings of the Muses and an early fireplace set with roundels, probably inserted in the early nineteenth century in Antiquarian taste.*

transomed windows here adapted later, so they soar from floor to ceiling (the ceiling is inserted), with stained glass removed from redundant churches. The screens support a minstrels' gallery, with an unplayable eighteenth-century chamber organ. The chimneypiece (perhaps from the Stephens's house at Eastington) is set with a black marble plaque as a medallion in a wreath of bay leaves, with escutcheons to the Stephens family. Beyond is the Jacobean Oak Room, the parlour of the Elizabethan house; the wainscoting and four panels of the Muses below the Tree of Life, dated 1627, seem to be a jumble of elements introduced later. An earlier fireplace dates to the time of Richard Stephens, the owner from 1587–99. The Ireton Room upstairs is hung with Flemish verdure tapestries of the mid-seventeenth century on the theme of the Quixote, and is one of several rooms to claim Cromwellian associations.

Above: *Alluring textures in the room where Cromwell reputedly slept in 1648, hung with coarse-weave Flemish tapestries of stylised sylvan scenes with landscapes, c.1640.*

Left: *The Elizabethan great hall has a chimneypiece inlaid with swags and black marble cartouches, perhaps removed from another Stephens's house in Eastington.*

At the rear of the house is the Edwardian west wing, with a floor area nearly equal to the old house itself, added in a muscular Neo-Tudorbethan by the Yorkshire architect J. T. Micklethwaite in 1904–05, to accommodate a ballroom and the rambling domestic offices of the Edwardian era. There is a freestanding chapel outside, cobbled together from architectural fragments in the early nineteenth century, including a Norman early font found on the estate. The tower is festooned with architectural bric à brac, apparently conceived as a folly.

Chavenage belonged, like Sudeley Castle and neighbouring Beverston, to Princess Goda, the sister of Edward the Confessor and wife to Earl Godwin. It became the property of Horsley Priory after the Conquest, a cell of the Abbey in Bruton in Somerset. At the Dissolution it was granted, with many other estates in the Cotswolds, including Sudeley, to the Protector Seymour. When Seymour lost his head under Edward VI, Chavenage passed to Sir Walter Denys, owner of Dyrham; in 1564, Sir Walter's son, Richard, sold the estate with the manor of Horsley to Edward Stephens of Eastington.

The existing house was built by him and has been owned by just two families. The Stephens family were feudal lords in Gloucestershire from the reign of Henry II. Branches of the family owned extensive land in the South Cotswolds, from Lypiatt and Eastington to Little Sodbury and Lyegrove. The Stephens family seem to have lived mainly at Eastington, and Chavenage may have been a minor seat, which explains why the main front externally has been little altered since Elizabethan times.

Nathaniel Stephens, owner from 1608 to 1660, was a Member of Parliament and fought in the Civil War, becoming an influential colonel in the Cromwellian army. He was a man of moderate opinions, however, and Cromwell is said to have sent his son-in-law, General Henry Ireton (a relation by marriage of Colonel Stephens), to Chavenage over Christmas 1648 in order to persuade him to consent to the King's 'removal'. Nathaniel was dithering in indecision when he was apparently warned by his father's ghost to have no part in the regicide. When Stephens finally acquiesced, he was cursed with a long catalogue of weird happenings, culminating in a lingering and ultimately fatal illness.

The last Stephens to live here was Henry Willis Stephens, a man of antiquarian tastes, who inherited in 1801, a bachelor and local clergyman who fled to take up with the Dominicans in Tenerife. Before his departure, he had added the billiard room and bay windows on the south garden front, and it is probably he who imported a host of architectural antiques now incorporated into the fabric, and altered the house in an advanced Neo-Jacobean taste. But by the mid-nineteenth century, the estate was heavily mortgaged to R. S. Holford, the rich owner of Westonbirt nearby, and was bought by a friend of the family, George Williams Lowsley Hoole-Lowsley-Williams in 1891.

Chavenage is still owned by his descendants. In 1970, David Lowsley-Williams discovered in the attic a portfolio of watercolours prepared for King George IV, which illustrated plans for the redecoration of Windsor Castle, the sale of which to the Royal Collection funded the repair of the roof.

Ireton's Room, hung with Flemish verdure tapestries on the theme of the adventures of Don Quixote, c.1640.

Little Sodbury Manor, Gloucestershire

Little Sodbury is the perfect Cotswold manor house, perched on a ledge half way up a hill, with views westerly over the wide expanse of the Severn Vale as far as the Welsh hills. A spectacular Iron Age hill fort looming above the chimney-stacks commands an early defensive site, sheltering the manor house from the east wind: this is probably 'Sodda's bury', whose name lives on in the three places named Sodbury. A few fragments of the old church, dedicated to the obscure Saint Adeline, patroness of weavers, survive in the garden.

It was here according to the chroniclers that the army of the Yorkists, under the future Edward IV, camped before the battle of Tewkesbury in May 1471. Possibly its leaders dined in the impressive hall. It remains, as it has been since then, the heart and kernel of the house, and the best of its date in the region. Dated to the early fifteenth century, it is still happily adapted to dining and hospitality. It is open to the roof, steeply pitched and impressively timbered with four tiers of wind braces, moulded purlins, and collar beams. The trusses spring from corbels in the form of angel heads, and high up on the east wall a grotesque mask (probably not *in situ*), like the one at Great Chalfield, forms a peep-hole squint. The lofty height and scale (about 42ft x 23ft) quite takes the breath away. Here a recent owner, Mark Harford, would dispatch intruding jackdaws at a fair range with his shotgun. The Gothic screens are rare in the Cotswolds as substantially original work. They have a studded partition over, enclosing a delightful oak-panelled bedroom. The Gothic porch leading to the garden, buttressed outside, has a massive beam to bar the door and again a cosy panelled porch room.

Above: *The main front faces west over the Severn Vale, terraces descending to a bowling green below. The hall range is behind the Gothic porch in the centre.*

Right: *The north-west range leading up to the great hall, as altered by Harold Brakspear.*

At the dais end it is much altered, with an oriel added by Sir Harold Brakspear who rebuilt whatever remained of the solar range to the north. There is evidence of little oriel rooms with an upper storey, which projected from both sides of the hall, balancing the porch on the main elevation.

The rest of the house has grown and adapted by accretions, like so many early houses, and its history, with wings upgraded and demolished over so many centuries, is hard to unravel. It certainly has early origins, but the hall which stands today is reasonably intact, built for the Stanshawe family about 1420. Their medieval house may have been laid out to an irregular courtyard plan, and a stray gatehouse doorway from this phase, integrated into a later plan, survives to the south.

In 1491, the house came by marriage into the possession of John Walsh of Olveston, a minor courtier as Receiver for the Berkeley estates, who prospered exceedingly by his connections. It was his son who was King Henry VIII's champion at the Coronation of 1509. Henry visited the house with Anne Boleyn in August 1535, when they are said to have watched a joust from the first-floor window, a fine oriel with a pierced parapet, which seems to have been added by Sir John Walsh at the same time as the domestic range running south from the hall.

Little Sodbury is remembered in history as the place where the great William Tyndale (1496–1536), Protestant scholar, linguist and reformer, was tutor (from about 1521) to Sir John's children. An austere bedroom, with timber-studded walls, claimed as his is shown in a garret. It was while at Little Sodbury that he set his ambition to translate the whole of the New Testament and much of the Old into the vernacular. His translation was to become one of the most influential works in English literature and to form the basis of the Authorised Version. Eventually, after being tried for heresy and treason, he was condemned to death by strangling. His monument (1866) at North Nibley is a landmark for miles around.

The house came next into the hands of Thomas Stephens, who purchased the manor to add to his substantial Gloucestershire landholdings (including Chavenage) in 1608, divided at his death between his three sons. Edward Stephens' portion included Lyegrove, near Badminton, and the two estates remained in the same ownership for several generations. He added a good staircase and early-seventeenth-century plasterwork, framed by pilasters and panels, in upstairs bedrooms, and chimneypieces. The Stephens favoured their seat Lyegrove after 1820.

The soaring hall, dated about 1420, has windbracing and an impressive close-studded partition above the screens.

The house exposed to the prevailing westerlies has suffered at the mercy of a succession of natural disasters. A fireball rolled its way into the great parlour in 1556 killing the Lord of the Manor, Maurice Walsh, and seven of his children who were with him. In 1703, the house was struck by lightning again, and the north (today's entrance) wing was damaged. The whole wing has been rebuilt, so there is little evidence of the medieval solar range it replaced, and the fenestration and planning are regular and Classical.

But the house was to decline through the following two centuries, until it was reduced to a rather profitless tenant farm by the late nineteenth century, and photographs show it was all but derelict by 1913. It was rescued in the nick of time by Lord Hugh Grosvenor, who appointed the skilful Sir Harold Brakspear (working at the time on Great Chalfield nearby) to restore and adapt the house in 1913–15. Grosvenor was killed in the War without living to benefit, and his kinsman, Baron de Tuyll, took over. Brakspear largely rebuilt the north wing solar range, particularly the east end of it, which now forms the entrance front in a rather cheerless Edwardian style, matching up what survived of the early-eighteenth-century work (to the west). Inside it forms a well-proportioned drawing room, entrance hall, with comfortable bedrooms over.

The Harford family bought the estate in 1952, and were succeeded in the 1980s by the Lampson family, of Atlantic Telegraph fame, the Lords Killearn. The house is much loved, and full of life and care. They have gallantly improved and restored the gardens and old bowling green, together with acres of magnificent retaining walls in drystone. Today the garden falls away in steep terraces with a succession of pools descending to a boating lake at the lowest level, which has been cleaned out and dredged.

Right: *One of the evocative oak-panelled bedrooms, remodelled by the Stephens family of Lyegrove in the early seventeenth century.*

Below: *The well-proportioned drawing room was created by Brakspear in 1913–15 in the then derelict solar range.*

Owlpen Manor, Gloucestershire

Owlpen Manor stands in its own remote valley under the edge of the Cotswolds, its desmesne of pasture and meadowland enclosed by an amphitheatre of steeply rising hills crowned with beech woods. Here the pearl-grey manor house, with its enormous yews and attendant outbuildings – church, court house, barns and mill – nestle under the lee of a steep hillside. They form a remarkable group, with a charm, a presence and a perfection of form and scale, which have long been admired as one of the treasures of the Cotswolds. The Tudor manor house was built and rebuilt between about 1450 and 1719 – since when, apart from the minor alterations in the early eighteenth century, nothing has been done, or more remarkably, undone.

Left: *View of the gables of the Jacobean west wing from the loggia below the gazebo.*

Above: *The south front between yews has evolved from east to west over nearly three centuries, from 1450 (right) to 1616 (left), with alterations in 1719. Through the long continuity of the Cotswold vernacular tradition, all are in harmony.*

There was a long century of decline, when Owlpen became a Sleeping Beauty house, abandoned and derelict, overwhelmed by magnificent yews and the growth of rampant ivy. The Stoughton family had inherited in 1815, having come into money in the early nineteenth century through their interests in Monmouthshire iron and coal. They built an Italianate mansion a mile away, at the other end of the estate, to the designs of Samuel Sanders Teulon, in about 1848. As the century progressed, Tudor and vernacular architecture began to be appreciated under the inspiration of the Arts and Crafts movement, and they had the means to keep up the garden as a place for excursions, installing a caretaker living in some back rooms. The house is described as 'quaint' and 'curious', when it was rediscovered by the Victorian Romantics, and in particular *Country Life*. It was first written up in 1906 by H. Avray Tipping, who described it as by then 'a garden house

more than anything else … making its brave fight against consuming Time.'

The place name is Saxon, meaning 'Olla's pen', after a ninth-century thegn, or headman. Owlpen was a possession throughout the Middle Ages of the de Olepenne family, who probably derived their name from the place, and who are recorded from the twelfth century as henchmen to their overlords, the Berkeleys of Berkeley Castle. To the last of the medieval de Olepennes we owe the west wing of the present house, with cruck trusses in the roof, similar to those in the great barn.

The male line failed about 1464, when the manor came into the Daunt family, following the marriage of Margery de Olepenne to Thomas Daunt, of a clothier family long settled in Wotton-under-Edge. The Daunts built most of what we see of the manor today, which grew by accretions from east to west over the three centuries to 1719. The hall/great chamber block in the centre is ascribed to Christopher Daunt, who inherited in 1542, following his marriage to Alice Throckmorton. The entry is at the lower end, where the screens would have been, and inside there are heraldic wall paintings commemorating the Daunts and de Olepennes.

The most recent part of the manor is the west wing, an extension at the upper end of the hall. This is the parlour/solar block, with a storeyed bay window, diagonal-clustered chimneys, and two gables to the west front, and a date stone: 'TD 1616'. Thomas Daunt II's Oak Parlour represents the lord's parlour at the upper end of the hall, with the solar over at first-floor level, confirming the tenacity and continuity of medieval arrangements in the Renaissance period at the manorial level.

The south front is of three gables, representing three centuries of evolution. It is asymmetrical, haphazard, yet 'illogically satisfactory' in its appeal, as James Lees-Milne noted. David Verey commented that it is one of those houses which has 'been altered so much at so many different periods

Above: *The painted cloth hangings in Queen Margaret's Room are a rare survival, dated about 1700, with scenes from the life of Joseph. The cabinet is by Sidney Barnsley, 1913.*

Right: *The small panelled drawing room created within the shell of the medieval service wing seen through an early Georgian doorcase, both 1719.*

that is difficult to say that this is Elizabethan more than anything else.' Christopher Hussey, writing in *Country Life* in 1952, was the first to recognise that it expresses a conventional, but squat, H-plan hall house, with cross-wings of unequal length at either end of the hall, a passage at first-floor level connecting them, and twin newel stairs. The Daunts had acquired considerable land in Co. Cork from the 1590s, a castle rather than a manor, and Owlpen declined to a mainland base and was little altered.

The final phase is one of the early-eighteenth-century improvements, well documented from 1719 onwards when Thomas Daunt IV inherited. He laid out the present terraced gardens. There is an emphasis on increasing Classicism and symmetry, and the insertion of sash windows, hearths,

Left: *The west wing, with its storeyed bay window and embattled parapet, is dated 'TD 1616' – for Thomas Daunt. It forms the parlour/solar block, the most recent part of the H-plan manor house.*

Below: *Sixteenth-century double doorway leading to the great chamber and the cross-passage, an advanced feature at this level.*

panelling and partitions in a general remodelling, restricted to the two main floors of the (early) east wing. The house was little used or occupied after his death in 1749, when the manor began its long decline, which has preserved the house almost as he left it.

The condition of the 'beautiful ancient manor house at Owlpen' had already aroused the concern of antiquarians by 1912. Edward Hudson and H. Avray Tipping, respectively founder-editor and Architectural Editor of *Country Life*, Thackeray Turner, Chairman of the Society for the Protection of Ancient Buildings, F. W. Troup and A. R. Powys, two successive secretaries of the Society, Ernest and Sidney Barnsley and Alfred Powell, architects of the Sapperton group in the Cotswolds, were all manoeuvring behind the scenes to persuade Thomas Anthony Stoughton II's widow, Rose, now Trent-Stoughton, to make urgent repairs: 'The roof is propped up from the floor joists below and [there is] a serious fissure, reaching from the top of one of the gables to within a few feet

of the ground', wrote A. R. Powys. Failing that, he was suggesting that the property be given to the National Trust, when 'it might be possible to raise a sum for its repair.'

Conditions deteriorated through the First World War, and the Troubles in Ireland, where the main family estates were, took their toll. Sidney Barnsley wrote to A. R. Powys at the SPAB on 10 July 1921: 'It would be fatal if the house was ever again used as a dwelling place, as the alterations and repairs that would be necessary would mean its ruin – except of course if it was taken in hand by Weir and somebody could be found appreciative enough to sacrifice modern ideas of comfort!'

Such was the condition – shuttered and forsaken, yet picturesque in its timelessness – of the manor house when Norman Jewson (1884–1975), a colleague of William Weir, first stumbled across it on one of his bicycle excursions from Sapperton. In July 1925, Jewson succeeded in buying Owlpen at auction with its old garden, orchards, gardener's cottage, mill, barn and outbuildings for £3,200. He was competing against Charles Wade, the eccentric collector who (in 1919) had bought Snowshill Manor, near Broadway. The few remaining contents had also been sold, including the village stocks, old dog spits, and Queen Margaret of Anjou's reputed bed and chair. With his sound knowledge and sureness of touch, Jewson's sensitive repair of Owlpen succeeded in capturing the spirit of place as well as texture and period.

For aftercomers like Christopher Hussey, Owlpen was a dream made real, crystallising the spirit of the secret valleys of the Cotswolds, and preserving, with all the substance of its structure and history, something of a dream's lovely unreality. Hussey was a regular visitor, who had first seen Owlpen before it was restored 'on a dark autumn afternoon in 1925', empty and sad behind its dripping barrier of yews in the bowels of the valley. He painted a number of sketches of Owlpen in his visiting albums at Scotney Castle; the *Country Life* articles came out in 1951.

My wife Karin and I acquired the house in 1974, and befriended Norman Jewson in his old age. When he died, he left his Arts and Crafts furniture and many of his papers to the house. His discovery and subsequent purchase and repair of Owlpen is usually considered his most enduring achievement.

The manor house and terraced hillside garden from the south, with the topiary yew parlour. It nestles below the church, heavily Victorianised, with the early Stuart summer house, to the left, and the early Georgian gate piers and segmental steps on an axis, to the right.

Snowshill Manor, Gloucestershire

Snowshill, pronounced 'Snozzle' locally, is a house more notable for what it contains than the distinction of its elevations or its story. It is the expression of an owner. Today it houses a collection put together by Charles Paget Wade (1883–1956), architect and artist-craftsman. He was an uncommonly eccentric dilettante of scholarly habits, a self-styled poet, who had money behind him to indulge his tastes and collecting habit from family sugar plantations in St Kitts, in the West Indies. He grew up at Yoxford in Suffolk, and spent his life from the age of seven accumulating things, a gallimaufry of bibelots, proven by the 22,000 items which today fill his house.

They form an unusual arcanum of curiosa: craft objects steeped in the inflections of social history or exotic provenances, heterodox, random, deconstructed, seldom informed by any aesthetic as formal works of art or integrity as a collection. They include musical instruments and Samurai swords and armour, heraldic cartouches blazoned with bright tinctures, exotic Balinese masks, Middle Eastern metalwork, farm bygones like butter moulds and cow bells – all in arrangements contrived by Wade like a studied picture hang in rooms of haunting gloom.

As a sapper in the Royal Engineers, stationed at Doullens in France, Wade saw the house in an advertisement in *Country Life*. He bought the house in 1919, partly attracted by the dereliction into which it had fallen, and started to fill it with his magpie collection. He toyed with and improved the house with panelling and architectural antiques, at the same time decorating surfaces with his rambling inscriptions. By 1924, he was already restless and made a bid to buy

Right: *The Classical entrance through gate piers to the south with cross windows was added by William Sambach sometime after 1712. His coat of arms is in the pediment over the door.*

Below: *'Dragon', where the fire belches smoke night and day, furnished with heraldic cartouches and balustrading, is set in the lower part of the medieval hall.*

Owlpen Manor. But he remained at Snowshill until 1956, leaving it to the care of the National Trust in 1951, before retiring to the West Indies.

Today, Snowshill is an Aladdin's den, with fragments of ships, figureheads or sailors' models whittled out of flotsam, Sicilian reliquaries, decorative painted banners, Victorian velocipedes and toys expressing the forgotten technologies of Midland factories, musical instruments, ubiquitous textiles and costumes – the conservator's nightmare. The names Wade called his rooms suggest nautical speak from his Atlantic crossings – 'Admiral', 'Top Gallant' (a garret under the eaves), 'Meridian' – or whimsical fantasies of a benign and blissful Arcadia – 'Seraphim' and 'Seventh Heaven'. A small room in the bowels beyond the hall he called 'Nadir', erecting a wagon-vaulted ceiling. 'Dragon', the lower part of the medieval hall, was where he kept a cheering fire night and day.

Above: *Everywhere cabinets and surfaces are crammed with clutter and curiosities, here in a south room panelled* c.1720.

Left: *The grim Samurai warriors in their armour are a popular exhibit in the vast collection of over 22,000 items.*

As he filled the house to the gunwales with extravagant clutter, Wade soon forced his own withdrawal to a medieval outbuilding across the garden, originally a brewery or dairy, which he called the Priest's House. There he set up his workshop and choice items from his collection, including his favourite fireside rocking chair. He became a reclusive alchemist in this den, transmuting objects by his strange art, and reserving the house for his occasional guests and his burgeoning collection.

Lutyens described him as 'a most remarkable creature, with a face like a death mask of Henry Irving with a thick fuzz of grey hair, cut like a sponge.' James Lees-Milne remembers him thus: 'He wore a stiff winged collar, was always in breeches and stockings, and his shoes were adorned with large silver buckles. With his old wax complexion, his presence was daunting. But at heart he was a child.'

The house is beautiful but not distinguished, a Cotswold manor house of the early modern period, set in a terraced garden on the hillside, near Broadway. It lies exposed to the snow down a narrow lane, affording hopeless access for the

hoards of summer visitors on timed tickets today. The front door is approached between gate piers. The Georgian façade built by the owner (post 1712), William Sambach, has an uncompromising fault line, with mullioned and transomed windows in stone on the right and over the pedimented doorway, while the left has sash windows of the period.

The building dates back to the fifteenth century, when it was a possession of the Abbey of Winchcombe (from as early as 821). King Henry VIII gave it to Katherine Parr at the Dissolution. The main block is a small hall house dating to about 1500, but was remodelled in the early seventeenth century, with an extension to the south and the insertion of upper rooms; Sambach's Classical details date to a third phase, c.1720. Inside it is a tenebrous rabbit warren where twenty-one rooms are shown, crammed full, and illuminating.

Wade designed the terraced garden as a series of outdoor rooms descending a south-west slope, in collaboration with Arts and Crafts architect M. H. Baillie-Scott, who had been a fellow pupil at the practice of the town planners, Parker & Unwin, working on Hampstead Garden Suburb. He dug terraces and ponds between 1920 and 1923 on the site of the old farmyard, laid out with architectural antiques again – a Venetian well head, and an armillary sphere, a bellcote, a Madonna, a zodiac clock – and gates and timber features painted his favourite blue.

Above: *One of the early Jacobean bedrooms inserted above the hall.*

Right: *The terraced gardens were laid out by Charles Wade, the magpie collector, with the help of his colleague M. H. Baillie-Scott in the early 1920s.*

Newark Park, Gloucestershire

Sir Nicholas Poyntz of Iron Acton was a courtier to Henry VIII (and his distant kinsman through Elizabeth Woodville) and a Member of Parliament for Gloucestershire, who served a spell in prison only because he was a dangerously close adherent to the Protector Somerset. His motto was: 'I obey whom I must, I serve whom I please, and I am what I merit.' He obeyed and served in his own way, and survived. In the end, his merit was not unrewarded: he was granted a quarter of the estate of Kingswood Abbey in February 1540, including the lands of Newark.

According to John Smyth, writing near the events in the 1620s, Sir Nicholas Poyntz built a house at Newark, Ozleworth, in the time of King Edward VI 'partly with the stones and timber of the demolished monastery of Kingswood, scarce two miles distant, and partly with the stones pulled from the crosses in the parishes thereabouts.' Sir Nicholas seems to have had little reverence for churchyard crosses, and was famous among his contemporaries for his incontinence. John Aubrey remarks acidly that he built a hunting lodge at Iron Acton 'to keep his Whores in'. Newark is precisely his 'New Work' for sylvan sports of various kinds, on a new site, already shown on Saxton's map of 1577. It was complete by the time he made his will in 1556, when he left his wife Dame Joan (a daughter of Thomas, the 5th Lord Berkeley) his 'new house at Osilworth that standith upon the hill and the parke that the same house standith in.'

Newark is therefore a courtier house where we might expect to see the latest architectural fashions displayed.

Right: *The house stands spectacularly on the edge of a sheer cliff overlooking the open valley to the south. This view shows Newark remodelled by Wyatt as a Neo-Gothic villa in the 1790s, set in its Picturesque landscape.*

Below: *The Tudor Renaissance front of Sir Nicholas Poyntz's hunting lodge of c.1550 has a progressive pedimented entrance (reset) with Doric columns; the parapet crenellation was added by James Wyatt.*

Functionally, it was not conceived as a dwelling house at all, nor (principally) a seraglio, but as a hunting lodge: a *maison de plaisance*. Probably, like Lodge Park, the roof served also as a grandstand, a vantage point from which to watch the chase. It is hidden in what still seem like infinite woods, wilderness in its day. Here Giles Daunt of Owlpen, with his fellow huntsman George Huntley of Boxwell (and Woodchester) and stalkers armed with 'nets and dogs', claimed to have slaughtered 231 foxes in one year.

It was recently discovered that the pedimented doorway on the east main front is not *in situ*. It is an advanced Italianate feature, where the proto-Renaissance mood was for the first time penetrating the Cotswolds. Here we see a new building in the latest style, four storeys tall, where a calm symmetry has overtaken the rambling medieval arrangement of Sir Nicholas's other house at Iron Acton (see page 34), forming a fully integrated plan and elevations. There is a central bay, and battlements (the crenellated parapet is probably an addition by Wyatt), evoking the strife of Venus and venery. The feeling is compact, in a style that echoes gatehouse architecture, prefiguring some of the great Tudor houses of the Smythson school, like Wootton Lodge in Staffordshire. Yet it remains, in Tipping's own phrase, 'a classic veneer upon a Gothic framework.'

Inside, the service rooms were in the semi-basement. The ground floor had two entertainment rooms. The first floor was one open space, as a well-lit banqueting room. Above, no doubt, were the bedroom apartments. The original roof, providing the viewing platform, may have had corner turrets. The present staircase is a Wyatt insertion – the original one would have been housed in a projecting staircase tower at the rear, as at Iron Acton Court.

Newark was adapted later as a functional country house, for it has three phases of evolution, each marked by changes in ownership. First it served as the Poyntz courtier hunting lodge, a plain symmetrical block of the Renaissance; second as the Lowe family's gentry manor house of the mid-seventeenth century, extended in an L-plan, with a parallel block, more typically Cotswold, which had twelve hearths in 1672; and third as the Reverend Lewis Clutterbuck's Gothic villa of c.1790, with appendages, ornament, lodges, new driveway and Picturesque landscaping by James Wyatt.

Wyatt's work was thorough and marks the building today, and its sash windows of the five-bay south front have some of the best views in England. The interior feel is predominantly of this Picturesque Neo-Gothic layer of its history, which has obscured the Tudor plan and details, made plain here and there by masonry scars, windows in strange places, stone laid bare in the restoration. Wyatt's scheme is at its most splendid in the entrance hall, with a screen of Doric columns and a bucranium frieze, and the staircase now set in the oriel bay to the east, with stained glass (*c.*1800).

Above: *The sylvan view to the south from the rooftops is reckoned one of the finest in the country.*
Left: *The centre of James Wyatt's south front, with its canted Gothic porch.*

Newark went through a long, steady decline in the twentieth century, and was almost lost to history. It went unnoticed by the early-twentieth-century writers of *Country Life*, like Tipping and Hussey. It was institutionalised after being bequeathed with an 800-acre estate to the National Trust in 1949, and accepted as a source of agricultural rent. James Lees-Milne, who dedicated his life to preserving great houses, admitted to having no eye for its architectural value. He proposed removing the roof and making of it a mighty and spectacular ruin on the hilltop where it stands, open to the sky.

Fortunately, this never happened. A prince came in the form of a dedicated Texan named Robert Parsons, an Anglophile architect, who took a long repairing lease of the desolate and cheerless house in 1972. With the labour of his own hands, and braving discomfort as he struggled with the ancient fabric, the weather and officialdom, he breathed new life into the house over a couple of decades of heroic work, patiently resurrecting it as a labour of love from a long century of decay. He uncovered bit by bit a rare masterpiece of the English early Renaissance. He furnished it appropriately and instituted a frank reign of hospitality.

The National Trust belatedly woke up to the repolished loveliness of the jewel that they owned, and it is now open to the public, with its garden cascading in terraces down the hillside, a glory of snowdrops in the spring.

THE JACOBEAN MANOR HOUSE

The Tudor house, still a hall house close to its medieval antecedents, fades often imperceptibly into the Jacobean. This is marked in the Cotswolds by a nascent vernacular Classicism, when correct Renaissance detail and symmetry have come of age. The Cotswolds do not possess the great prodigy houses of the courtiers and London merchants, but its best Jacobean manor houses are worthy gems, raised by local squires and wool men. These are often compositions grouped with outbuildings of quality, exemplified by Stanway and its gatehouse, set in their deep valleys on the edge of the Cotswolds. The Jacobean house marks the advent of careful planning to a compact design. The hall was gradually demoted from the hierarchical medieval hall, with the raised dais, to an entrance hall, and private dining parlours as separate rooms. The following houses have been selected to show the range of fine Jacobean houses in the region.

Above: *Jacobean Doughton Manor (of 1632–41), outside Tetbury, was probably the old manor of the village, across from the Prince of Wales's Highgrove. It was carefully repaired by Norman Jewson in 1933.*

Left: *Asthall Manor, near Burford, built for Sir William Jones c.1620, viewed across the water meadows of the Windrush: the quintessence of the Cotswold manorial group.*

Upper Swell Manor, near Stow-on-the-Wold, unusually for the popular Cotswolds, was until recently untouched and abandoned, in the care of the church. It represents the manor of Evesham Abbey, standing near the church. The existing house is dated about 1630. It is not a dwelling house, but closer in character to a lodge, like Newark Park and Lodge Park. There is strong central emphasis, with a gable above the two-storey porch, its outstanding feature, all in cut stone. This is a riot of Tuscan columns and strapwork frieze, with the segmental pediment broken by a shield bearing the arms of the Stratford family. Inside, a stair leads up by the porch to a richly decorated upper room, with a frieze of plaster sphinxes and an outstanding Renaissance hooded chimney-piece with fish-scale ornament, and a good balustered staircase.

Stanton Court, near Broadway, a few miles north of Stanway, dates to around 1620. Between 1906 and 1937, the village was maintained by a model squire, the architect Sir Philip Stott, as a neat paragon of Cotswold vernacular, and it is described by Pevsner as the finest village, architecturally, in the North Cotswolds. Stott improved the house, removing all traces of Georgian accretions and tactfully substituting them for 'correct' Neo-Jacobean restorations.

Here the doorway in the porch is set to the side, and the hall has migrated to the centre of the main front, so that the principle of symmetry in plan and elevation, by now sacrosanct for this quality of house, is not offended. The main (entrance) façade has flanking gabled wings which project either side of the hall. In the centre are three gables: a porch and hall bay window respectively are formed in extruded angles, as narrow tower blocks either side of the hall.

Doughton Manor, of 1632–41, is three miles from Tetbury, on the high Cotswolds, opposite the Prince of Wales's house at Highgrove, and was probably always the old manor of the village, mentioned in 1328. It is a conservative Jacobean country house typical of the Cotswold vernacular, with unusually thick walls (so thick that they were once said to be made of cob), built modestly in rendered rubble with stone windows and dressings, and a central stone porch.

The house is H-plan, with the front and back façades almost identical, both with five tall gables. They are still timidly asymmetrical, so that the exterior elevations express the hierarchy of the uses of the rooms within, in the medieval fashion. One of the flanking wings contains the kitchens and service rooms, with plain windows; the other contains the parlours, with grander bay windows on the main front. The entry by the porch is just off centre, with the larger section containing the hall. The chimney shafts have been truncated as ungainly stumps; the stacks are built into the walls.

Top left: *Campden House, Chipping Campden. The east banqueting house in cut stone, with its Renaissance arcaded windows, strapwork cresting and fine twisting chimneys, was made habitable by the Landmark Trust in 1989.*

Above: *Many-gabled Stanton Court, near Broadway, was carefully restored by Sir Philip Stott in the early twentieth century. The entrance is set to the side in a narrow tower block, so as not to offend the principles of symmetry.*

Right: *The flanking gate lodges to Campden House are virtually all that remains of the Cotswolds' grandest Jacobean prodigy house, built by Sir Baptist Hicks and destroyed in the Civil War by Prince Rupert. It had stood for barely twenty-five years.*

Inside, the great chamber has a two-stage, heraldic chimney-piece, with strapwork cartouches bearing the Talboys' arms, the designs of which can be traced to sources in engravings by the Italian Benedetto Battini, according to Nicholas Cooper. The builder was Richard Talboys, a wool man from Yorkshire, who bought the estate of just 4 acres in 1631 in order to build a country house, away from his business in the smoke of Tetbury. The gate piers to the north bear his mark: 'R.T. 1641'.

Doughton Manor later became a farmhouse, united in the same ownership as the grander house at Highgrove. Part of its appeal is that it has remained little altered. It was put into repair with admirable restraint for Colonel F. A. Mitchell by the Arts and Crafts architect Norman Jewson, in 1933.

Campden House in Chipping Campden was the nearest the Cotswolds approached to a Jacobean prodigy house. It was built about 1612–20 for Sir Baptist Hicks, an immensely rich London mercer in the King's favour, and rising, who in 1628 was created Viscount Campden of Campden, before dying the following year.

The house formed a complete and carefully planned ensemble with its pair of flanking banqueting houses, gate lodges, a terrace of alms houses, and superb gardens, set on the edge of the town. Fragments of the house can be detected above ground level, with the gateway and boundary walls. Four illustrations of the house 'before it was pulled down', all based on the same lost original, date from the eighteenth century. They record a symmetrical, three-storey, gabled house of eleven bays, with a complex and exotic roofscape of shaped gables and domes, and its ancillary buildings and terraced gardens with plots.

The house is reputed to have cost £29,000 to build and £15,000 to furnish. Sadly, it was to have a short innings as the 2nd Lord Campden, who died in 1643, and the 3rd Lord Campden declared their hand with the Royalists in the Civil War. After it had stood for hardly twenty-five years, the house was fired and then mostly dismantled on the orders of Prince Rupert in 1645 in order to make it useless for occupation by the Parliamentarian forces. It became a quarry later in the century, and was never rebuilt. A fragment of its main façade is all that remains.

The pair of banqueting houses, east and west, escaped the fire and destruction, and remain a marvel of their date, suggesting the glories which have been. They stood at either end of the terrace in front of the house, with their arcaded windows enclosing the loggias on the main floors. They have roofs with obelisks and trefoil ornament, and heavy, blind strapwork cresting, elaborate twisting corner chimneys, with ornamental finials, and a plaster frieze inside the west lodge. They are cut into the rising terraces, accessed at different levels from them; the lower rooms may have been fitted up as grottoes, like those at Woburn Abbey.

Top left: *Upper Swell Manor, near Stow-on-the-Wold, built as a* plaisance *in about 1630, with its central storeyed porch and segmental pediment.*

Above: *Bibury Court, built for Sir Thomas Sackville in 1633, retaining the earlier Elizabethan range (to the right). The interiors have been reordered, most notably in the early twentieth century for Sir Orme Clarke.*

Right: *Asthall Manor, near Burford, viewed across the churchyard; a typical Cotswold bale tomb stands at a drunken angle showing its Baroque* memento mori.

Earthworks survive as shapeless humps and banks in the pasture, representing the layout of a high-status Renaissance garden like that at Raglan Castle in Monmouthshire, advanced for its date. This has vanished from view but fortuitously survived unaltered underground, escaping the whims of subsequent fashion. Outlines of terraces, walks, a canal and water parterre and numerous early features were securely fossilised until they were deconstructed by archaeology and aerial photography in the 1980s. The old gatehouse and banqueting houses have recently been restored by The Landmark Trust and the barn has become a museum devoted to the Arts and Crafts.

Asthall Manor, near Burford in Oxfordshire, was built in 1620 for Sir William Jones to an H-plan in golden ashlar. One of the five gabled bays on the east front, facing the church, was added in 1916. During the First World War, the manor was used as a convalescent home. It became the Mitford house when Lord Redesdale bought it in 1919, moving from Batsford Park, near Moreton-in-Marsh (see page 186).

Lower Slaughter Manor, near Cheltenham, was granted to the senior branch of the Whitmore family of Shropshire in 1611, who only sold it in 1964. It is an advanced house, built in 1656 by Valentine Strong, whose contract for the work survives. It is one of the first Cotswold houses built to a double-pile plan, square, of five by five bays, with a hipped roof set to a pronounced overhang. But its Jacobean harmony has been spoiled by large extensions in the nineteenth century, particularly an awkward east wing of 1891.

Bibury Court is picturesquely set at the end of a short valley, on the edge of England's so-called most beautiful village. The main part of the house was built to an E-plan in 1633 for Sir Thomas Sackville, retaining an earlier projecting wing towards the church. The central porch is the strongest feature, with Renaissance doorway, Serlian rustication, and the arms of Sir Thomas and his wife. A good deal of internal remodelling was carried out: first in the mid-eighteenth century, then in 1830 for the 2nd Lord Sherborne by Lewis Wyatt, and finally there was an early-twentieth-century restoration in Neo-Georgian and Neo-Jacobean style undertaken for Sir Orme Clarke. Since 1968, the house has been a hotel, often floodlit at night.

Chastleton House, Oxfordshire

You approach the archway in front of Chastleton down the deep lanes of the Oxfordshire Cotswolds, not far from Moreton-in-Marsh, past a pretty dovecote, to find before you, soaring and solid, five, narrow, brooding gables of brown ochre stone, with a church set obligingly to one side. It is one of the most perfect Jacobean compositions in the country.

The history of the manor begins in 777 with Offa, King of the Mercians, who made a grant of land here to Evesham Abbey. It descended to the Catesbys, who owned the manor from the late medieval period. The last of them was Robert Catesby, the charismatic ringleader of the conspirators in the Gunpowder Plot, killed resisting arrest in 1605. Nothing remains of the medieval manor house which stood on the site.

Above: *The screens' end of the great hall in its 'Old English' arrangement, with contrived clutter, as photographed by Charles Latham in 1902.*

Left: *The entrance with strapwork pediment is set sideways, in the return wall at the lower end of the hall.*

Chastleton was built anew between 1607 and 1612 for Sir Walter Jones, son of a wool merchant from Witney, who had prospered at the Bar and was MP for Worcester. Though he had risen in status from trade to gentry, and proudly traced his descent from Priam of Troy, his descendants grew poorer and poorer over the following centuries, so the history of Chastleton has been uneventful and its fabric preserved virtually as he left it when he died in 1632. It makes its mark on history only once, for the codification of the rules of croquet, in 1868.

Sir Walter Jones's grandson, Arthur, was known as 'the Cavalier', as he supported the King's Royalists during the Civil War and suffered fines under the Commonwealth after he had escaped from the battle of Worcester. The Joneses continued to suffer as High Tory Jacobites in the eighteenth century.

Joneses were succeeded in 1828 by the Whitmores of Dudmaston in Shropshire. The descent moved sideways again

to Alan Clutton-Brock, sometime Art Correspondent of *The Times* and Slade Professor of Art, in 1955. He would shuffle to the door to show a handful of visitors round an arctic and increasingly dilapidated house. He greeted one through a miasma of alcohol and cobwebs, maintaining the cobwebs were cultivated, 'as they held the place together'.

He reigned in a time warp of donnish seclusion, among dank halls and the exquisite clutter of his ancestors, muffled in a greatcoat of heavy tweed, and spouting a charming patter à propos his Mannerist garden, or the romantic tale of the 'Cavalier' Arthur Jones in flight from the battle of Worcester in 1651. The Cavalier lurked in his secret place over the porch, while his wife laced a flagon of ale with a sleeping draught of laudanum for Cromwell's men who had come looking for him and were resting in the room next door. Jones stole the best of their horses and made his escape.

During Clutton-Brock's tenure, the rooms were unheated and musty, and increasingly bare as he consigned family heirlooms one by one to the London sale rooms. Clutton-Brock died in 1976 and his widow, Barbara, struggled on with the house and the remaining 30 acres of the estate. By the 1980s, the decay of this Jacobean treasure house was far advanced and imminent collapse threatened to condemn the house to history. Fortunately, the National Trust acquired the house in 1991. Since their stewardship, the house has been pulled apart and put together again exactly as it was, preserving the illusion that nothing has changed.

Chastleton stands with five tall gables sandwiched between the embattled staircase towers; the façade is articulated in five, advancing and receding planes, the towers, flanking bays, projecting bays and the tallest bay with the hall sitting tight in the centre all capped with small gables. The façade is studiously symmetrical, with bays for the porch and the hall oriel either side of the central hall. The front steps lead up disconcertingly to a blank wall, as the entrance is contrived sideways in the flanking return wall of the porch to conceal its off-centre position, as at Stanton Court. The windows are symmetrical, but jumbled, and stand together with their string courses out of level.

The plan is square, compact but complex, based on the central courtyard, here outward facing, with two staircase

Above: *The long gallery in the attic with plasterwork in low relief, an interlace of ribbons and roses, to the barrel-vaulted ceiling: 'one of the most glorious rooms in England'.*

Right: *The great chamber is the grandest reception room, with a riot of decoration smothering every surface: pendant bosses to the plaster ceiling, carved wainscoting, and a frieze of painted panels of sibyls and prophets.*

towers at either end of the hall. The Oak Parlour for daily family use is off the lower end of the hall, where the kitchen might have been under the Tudor arrangement. The principal entertaining rooms are on the first floor, approached up the grander of the two staircases, with obelisk finials, which leads off the upper end of the hall. They are situated in the north range, arranged in an enfilade of great chamber, withdrawing chamber and bedchamber. The magnificent long gallery on the top floor runs the whole length of the north range.

Walter Jones would have cultivated good contacts in London, and Mark Girouard has suggested that he sought the advice of an architect of national standing, such as the obscure Robert Smythson, architect of Hardwick Hall, Burton Agnes and Wollaton. The intermediary may have been his friend and neighbour Ralph Sheldon, who is known to have supplied tapestries for Chastleton and has his arms in a place of honour over the fireplace in the best bedroom. The building work at Chastleton is traditional Cotswold vernacular, executed by local masons.

The interiors are rich in textures and provenance, giving a sense of time arrested. Several items mentioned in a 1633 inventory, like the great oak table in the hall, are still *in situ*. The textiles are of quality, and authentic. The Fettipace Room, the grandest bedroom, is hung with Flanders tapestries of Jacob and Essau recorded in the house in 1633. The closet beyond is lined in rare Irish or flame stitch hangings of the seventeenth century. The striped wool wall hangings at the top of the east stairs are of a material known as dornix (from Tournai), universal in seventeenth-century inventories, but unknown today. Two Barcheston tapestries are displayed with the date 1595 and the initials of Walter and Elinor Jones.

The great chamber was the Jones's principal reception room, every surface of which is decorated with a provincial, restless virtuosity. The ceiling has vine trails, flowers, ribs and pendants. The walls are wainscoted, with painted panels of sibyls and prophets in the Roman manner framed in a frieze of caryatids. Allusive metaphysical conceits and references from Flemish pattern and emblem books inform the decorative arabesques. The heavy stone chimneypiece is the *tour de force*, with a strapwork cartouche whose armorial bearings express all too blatantly Jones's nouveau riche origins and gentry pretensions. The great chamber looks over the topiary garden, admired by the Victorians for the purity of its age. It reinforces the sense of organic timelessness, but may or may not be contemporary with the house.

The five narrow gables of Chastleton's main front in tawny stone (1607–12) project and recede alternately between the flanking staircase towers. It was taken over by the National Trust in 1991 after 400 years in the ownership of the Jones family, who built it.

Stanway House, Gloucestershire

Noble Stanway is to many the ideal of the English manor house. It is one of the glorious Cotswold groupings, in glowing ochre stone from Guiting, consisting of manor house, gatehouse, tithe barn and Norman church. The principal elements of this composition at the foot of the Cotswold escarpment, near Tewkesbury, have grown in harmony for over a thousand years, all of a piece. And Stanway has changed hands just once in that time.

It was given by the curiously-named thegns Odo and Dodo to the Abbots of Tewkesbury, perhaps as early as the date of its foundation in 715, and their 'fair stone house' was noted by John Leland. It came to Sir Richard Tracy, younger brother of the owner of Toddington, whose family, claiming descent from Charlemagne, had been settled in the area since before the Norman Conquest. Richard leased it from the monks in 1533, three years before the Dissolution of the smaller monasteries. His family have held it ever since, if by dint of a descent through the female line in 1817, when it came into the Charteris family, the Scottish Earls of Wemyss.

Sir Paul Tracy inherited in 1569 and started work some ten years later, raising up the house on earlier monastic foundations to an unusual L-plan, with a hall and service block in the west (entrance) range, and round the corner to the south, the long parlour block. Sir Paul's hall is the glory of the house, dominated within and without by a magnificent sixty-light oriel window, on a five-sided plan, at the dais end of the hall. Lady Cynthia Asquith, diarist and a daughter of the house, described the evening light 'filtering through the oriel, with hundreds of latticed panes, so mellowed by time that whenever the sun shines through their amber and green glass, the effect is a vast honeycomb ...'

Sir Paul Tracy was created a baronet, one of the first, in 1611, and died in 1620, when he was succeeded by Sir Richard

Above: *The medievalising Renaissance gatehouse of 1630–40 with a Mannerist centrepiece is set at an angle to the house. The three shaped gables are topped with the scallop shells of the Tracy family, whose descendants have lived here since the Reformation.*

Right: *The long south front round the corner of the same date. The highest fountain jet in Britain springs in Baroque water gardens under restoration on the hillside.*

Tracy, who was an inspired and innovative builder. He added the house's great triumph of the gatehouse of the early seventeenth century (c.1630), and remodelled the south range.

The gatehouse is a medievalising, early Renaissance hybrid, producing a storeyed extravagance with three, shaped gables set with the Tracy scallop shells, a decorative flourish repeated throughout in finials, seats and niches. It is placed not, as in other Tracy houses, such as Toddington and Sudeley, opposite the main (west) entrance, but at right angles to it. The approach to the house is mediated by its gateway, itself a medieval conception, giving the feeling of a stately ceremony of entry every time the courtyard is accessed.

The courtyard is enclosed by a north gateway standing beyond, a west boundary wall (on the churchyard side) and the house with its main door to the east. The bay windows rise to full height either side of the Mannerist centrepiece, the archway of which carries a segmental pediment broken by a panel framing the shield of the Tracy (and Atkyns) arms, again with a pediment. There are Classical details in an advanced style for its date, more so than the hall of fifty years earlier, such as caused it for many years to be attributed rather hopefully to Inigo Jones. Today, the architect is generally thought to be Timothy Strong, of the family of master masons from Great Barrington.

The south front is a long range with a strong horizontal emphasis that pulled the old work together behind an improved façade of seven bays, with mullioned and transomed windows. It is almost symmetrical, with an elegant doorway in the centre of 1724, probably added by Francis Smith, and arcaded strapwork cresting and battlements along the roof-line, answering that on the gatehouse bays.

Above: *Stanway's grouping in gold ashlar. The bay window with strapwork cresting c.1630 (right) is answered by the shaped gables of the contemporary gatehouse in Flemish Mannerist style, surmounted by the Tracy scallops against the sky. It stands across the long garden wall pierced by a* clairvoyée *forming peep-holes over the public road.*

Left: *The great hall dais is suffused with light from latticed casements in the oriel. The shuffleboard table (to the right) was made for the room in the 1620s.*

The old north-east stone range may have stood on the site of the medieval or early-sixteenth-century house, and was still standing when Kip executed his faithful engraving, c.1710. About 1859, it was demolished, when a new north wing, kitchen court and stables were added by William Burn. Detmar Blow also worked here in 1913, tidying, giving shape, and extending. Lord Wemyss demolished most of Burn's wing and back premises in 1948–54 to make the house 'viable'.

Inside, the improvements and adaptations over the generations since Jacobean times are more evident. The house is entered by the screens' passage, an early-eighteenth-century Doric colonnade of 1724 replacing the Jacobean arrangement. The great hall, lined with ashlar stone in the twentieth century, is hung with hatchments, antlers and tapestries. At the dais end is a table, with a single plank top scored with lines for the game of shuffleboard, 22ft-long, built for the room from timbers felled in 1620. The present dining or 'audit' room (still used for collecting rents) and old kitchen are off the lower end of the hall, to the north. The drawing room is approached up steps off the upper end, to the south, with early-Georgian panelling and a Neo-Jacobean ceiling of the 1860s.

After 1817, Stanway became a subsidiary of the Scottish estates of the Earls of Wemyss and March, descended from Susan Tracy Keck, last of the second dynasty of Tracys. In 1883, Lord Wemyss made it over to his son, Hugo, Lord Elcho, who had married Mary Wyndham. It became the centre of a glittering social and intellectual coterie, slightly at odds with the hunting squires of the Cotswolds. Their talented children formed the *jeunesse dorée* of the Edwardian era, when Stanway was the resort of a charmed aristocratic circle called 'The Souls'. They had an important influence on the cult of the Cotswold manor house, exemplified most resoundingly by Stanway. The house was restored by Detmar Blow, and featured in *Country Life* in November 1916.

The present owners are Lord and Lady Neidpath, who admirably maintain Stanway's traditions of munificent gentility. The Baroque water garden attributed to Charles Bridgeman has a formal canal of the 1730s, eight ponds, a pyramid, built by Robert Tracy in 1756 to commemorate his father, from which the cascade tumbles down the slope, and a fountain. Lord Neidpath restored these features and in June 2004 set in motion the highest fountain in Britain at 300 feet and the highest gravity-fed fountain in the world, supplied by a reservoir basin 580 feet up on the Cotswolds.

Cold Ashton Manor, Gloucestershire

Christopher Hussey summarised Cold Ashton in *Country Life*, December 1934, as 'a hill top house, grey gables pricking the sky. A perfectly integrated symmetrical composition.' It is one of the most assured Jacobean compositions in the Cotswolds, carefully if conservatively planned. The house is set exposed to the cold winds on the highest point of the Cotswolds here, dramatic, commanding spectacular views over hills and St Catherine's valley.

The manor of Cold Ashton belonged to Bath Abbey from the time of Athelstan to the Dissolution, when it was bought like many others by Sir Walter Denys, a speculator in monastic estates, for £760 11s. 8d. He sold the house on for an £80 profit to the Pepwell family, but the present house is believed to date from the purchase of the estate by John Gunning, Mayor of Bristol, in 1629. Sir Robert Gunning's arms are raised over the elaborate gateway from the road on cresting, flanked by fruitful urns, dating some time after his grant of arms in 1662.

H. Avray Tipping described the gateway as designed by a man who had studied his John Shute or some other Classical authority, 'the first English exposition of the Vitruvian rule' (1563): 'the rustication and restraint of the pilasters and entablature hint at a fairly direct Italian inspiration.'

The house is approached through its gateway arch up segmental steps, across a forecourt, where its façade rises above eleven more steps, with two, gabled cross-wings flanking the recessed centre: a Classical composition in Gothic dress. The wings have the canted bays of the Cotswolds; in the centre is a Classical balustrade over the porch, and a pair of oval windows either side. The north front is gabled and flush, resembling neighbouring Wick Court.

There is an entry set in its traditional place, at the lower end of the hall, which is to the rear. The hall screen is 'the chief jewel of this gem-like house', wrote Tipping. It is indeed the glory of the interior, richly carved, Classical, and exceptionally well preserved. The passage side away from the

Above: *The symmetrical south front whose grey gables prick the sky. The house on this hilltop site dates to shortly after 1629, with cross-wings and the typical canted bays of the Cotswolds.*

Right: *Looking along the screens' passage, 'the chief jewel' of the interior, to the gateway arch, surmounted by fruitful urns, dated after 1662.*

hall is the most elaborate, with fielded panels carved in the solid with gouged rustication. Two archways lead into the hall, which have Corinthian pilasters and dentil mouldings, and faint traces of polychrome paintwork.

Sir Robert was succeeded by the Langton family, later Gore-Langtons, who became Earls Temple of Stowe, seated more comfortably at Newton Park outside Bath, while they let Cold Ashton decline. They sold in 1902 to the sitting tenant, Mr Lucas, a yeoman farmer who continued to hold the estate until 1918, altering the house little. Cold Ashton was featured in its state of decay in the early *Country Life* of 1905.

Colonel Reggie Cooper was the saviour who acquired the house from Lucas and started to restore it with uncommon dedication and skill in 1923. He was certainly influenced by the cult of the manor house promulgated by Edward Hudson and H. Avray Tipping in the pages of *Country Life*. He was one of a group of repairers of early houses in the first years of the twentieth century, called by John Cornforth the 'ex-Foreign Office circle', gentlemen of independent means and exquisite taste, with a passion for buying early manor houses which had fallen into advanced decay

Reggie Cooper started to collect appropriate early furniture in oak and walnut to complement the house, and created at Cold Ashton another paragon of the Cotswold manor house, connected to its idealised past. Tipping saw reflected in the composition this ideal: 'Colonel Cooper, with unerring judgment, refrained from "restoration" and ... by mere repair and preservation gave back to the whole place, that is garden environment as well as house interior, the spirit of its past.'

Cooper continued to pursue his passion for early houses as a way of life, moving from Cold Ashton to Cothay in Somerset in 1925, a perfect example of the small, fifteenth-century manor house, where he laid out the existing gardens in the following years. Then he tackled Julians in Hertfordshire, and finally the fourteenth-century manor house of Knightstone in Devon. Cold Ashton was Cooper's first and perhaps one of his most successful restorations.

Left: *Rear of the house with the yew walk.*

Below: *View from the top of the house over the gateway into the wooded combes of St Catherine's valley.*

PANS LODGE
IN COLDBOURN GROUE
GLOS:SHIRE.
1757

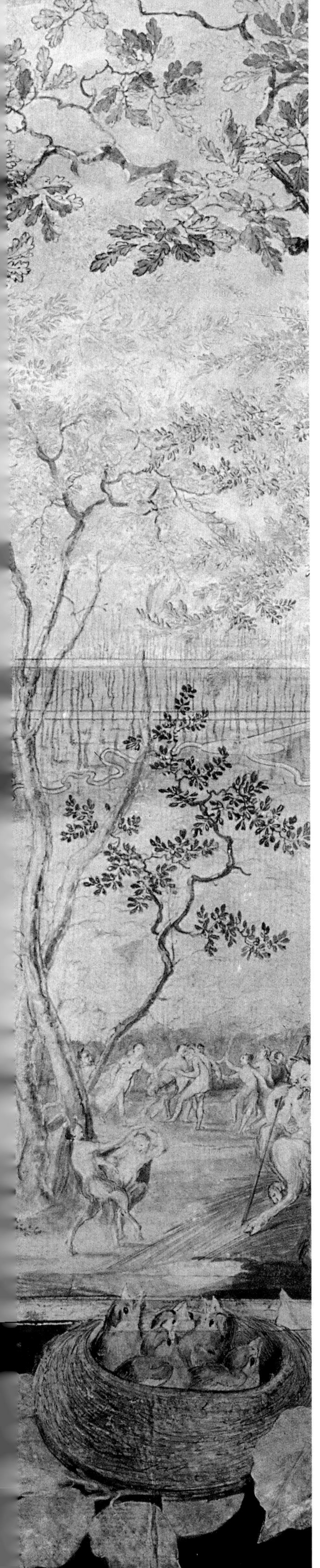

THE CLASSICAL HOUSE IN THE COTSWOLDS

There was a building boom in the Cotswolds following the Restoration in 1660. Nicholas Kingsley in *The Country Houses of Gloucestershire* Vol 2 counted 440 known building campaigns on Gloucestershire country houses from 1660 to 1830. The great Cotswold houses of this period owe their origins to royal connections and a new sense of aristocratic order: Badminton, Dyrham and Cirencester were built by politicians and loyal favourites at court. The nobility took up seasonal residence on their rural estates creating a need for houses in the latest taste, as they extended, rationalised and improved their demesnes. As a result, some of the most impressive landscape gardens of their day were created at these houses in the Cotswolds.

The nobility was emulated by the squirearchy of traditional landowners (or occasionally the rising mercantile class, at their

Above: *Bourton House, Bourton-on-the-Hill, probably rebuilt by a local architect on the foundations of an earlier house, 1708–10. The projecting single-bay wings mark the Jacobean corner towers which preceded them.*

Left: *View of Pan's Lodge with satyrs and revellers, a Gothic summer house near Bull's Cross (demolished before 1824) which looked over the valley to Painswick House. One of a series of paintings by Thomas Robbins the Elder, dating from 1748, which has provided the key to the complete re-creation of the Painswick Rococo garden since the late 1980s.*

most magnificent at houses like Northwick Park), often using metropolitan architects, who embarked on projects of rebuilding and rearranging houses. Such adaptations include: Barnsley Park (possibly John James, in the circle of the Duke of Chandos, 1719–31), Sherborne House (work by Kent, 1728; stables), Adlestrop (Sanderson Miller, 1750–63), Estcourt Park (probably by Thomas Estcourt, 1776) and Barrington Park (William Smith of Warwick, 1737–38). Broadwell Manor (1740s), Sandywell Park (c.1708, with later wings by Francis Smith, 1720s), Bourton House (c.1708) and Burnt Norton (probably designed by the owner, Sir William Keyte, c.1720) were all new houses on old estates.

The established squires and squarsons, and overwhelmingly the mill owners of the Stroud valleys, commissioned numerous projects to recreate a host of good quality gentry houses, often with design influences from Bath and Bristol, which reinforce the Cotswolds as the area with a greater density of listed buildings than any rural area in the country. The designs were mostly ascribed to unknown local architect-masons and include: Alderley Grange (c.1744), Ebworth Park (1731), Lypiatt Park, The Ridge (by G. S. Repton, c.1817), Stout's Hill (1752), Upton House (1752), Painswick House (1733–35), Castle Godwyn (1730s) and Beacon House, Highgrove House (1796–98) and Gatcombe Park (1770s, with additions by George Basevi in the 1820s).

Above: *Castle Godwyn is set in Paradise, built by a local builder-mason in the 1730s. It is one of many good mill owners' houses in the Stroud valleys.*

Left: *Painswick House, Painswick. The Rococo mood of the garden is captured by this view through a Gothic arch – one of at least 15 such garden features erected by the owner Benjamin Hyett from the 1740s.*

This was the period of compact, symmetrical houses enriched with Classical detail, when the double-pile plan established itself at houses like Fairford Park (demolished in 1957). The greatest houses are the notable exceptions to this plan: Badminton, Cirencester and Dyrham all follow the Tudor arrangement of one room deep.

Bourton House, at Bourton-on-the-Hill, was bought by Alexander Popham from the descendants of Sir Thomas Overbury, the poet and essayist 'unnaturally' murdered in one of the most sensational crimes in English history in 1616. It was rebuilt either for a later Thomas, or his son Edward, c.1708, probably by a local mason-architect of the Warwick school, and is described as 'a handsome large seat' by the historian Atkyns at that time. It was reared on the foundations of the older Jacobean house on the site, the corner towers of which are reincarnated in the present projecting single-bay wings, set as angle pavilions, which provide useful dressing rooms within. Both façades have giant, Ionic pilasters supporting a central pediment. Inside, there is sixteenth-century panelling and doors, possibly from the earlier house. There is a large stone barn of 1570, with trusses, and today a magnificent garden.

Among the many smaller Classical houses in the Cotswolds, Poulton Manor (1690s), near Cirencester, stands out as a charming village house, in a hybrid of Cotswold vernacular and grander precedents indicated by the handsome symmetry in plan and elevation. Nicholas Kingsley suggests John Bedwell (father or son) as the local builder. It stands full square, with mullioned and transomed windows, and a hipped roof with single dormer and prominent cornice, and has been little altered. In the attic, where its architect-owner Anthony Sandford had his drawing-board latterly, a massive arch carries the central chimney-stack. The drawing room is panelled, with original brass door furniture.

The earliest example of the Palladian style, with a 'cleaner' emphasis on composition, proportion and correct Classical precedent in detail, appears on the entrance front at Northwick Park, near Moreton-in-Marsh. The earlier west front had been built by an architect close to William Talman, c.1686, for Sir James Rushout, of a family of Flemish merchants based in London. The east entrance front (1728–30) was altered for Sir John Rushout, incorporating existing

elements, including the old corner towers (which have later shaped gables), to a design by the virtuoso Neo-Palladian and amateur, Lord Burlington. The famous art gallery was added in a new wing in 1832.

Barrington Park (1737–38) is the Cotswolds' purest Palladian house, associated with the circle of William Kent, though executed by William Smith the Younger of Warwick. It was built for Lord Talbot, raised on a terrace over the river Windrush, near Burford. The centrepiece has four, giant Corinthian pillars on a rusticated plinth, with pediment and balustraded parapet. The wings were added later, in 1873, by J. M. Anderson, who succeeded his uncle, William Burn, together with the staircase and billiard room. There are fine ceilings inside, with trophies and rich friezes, probably by Charles Stanley, an Anglo-Dane.

Alderley Grange (c.1744), Wotton-under-Edge, has a long, low entrance front set back from the village street, with rusticated Serlian windows in the centre of the façade over the door, and a heavy parapet, panelled and pedimented; the rear wing has the date stone 1608. It is sometimes attributed to Thomas Paty, one of six related Patys of a dynasty of Bristol contractor-architects, and was extended c.1810. It was the house of James and Avilde Lees-Milne from 1961 to 1975, who recreated the garden in a Sissinghurst manner, beautifully maintained by the present owners, Guy and the Hon. Camilla Acloque.

Beacon House, Painswick, opposite the famous churchyard, marks the site where beacons for signalling were lit in the Civil War. It was built for a Mr Wood in Palladian style (1767–69) and, like Alderley, is sometimes attributed to Thomas Paty. The interior is its glory, where a riot of English Rococo plasterwork decoration, with Pan's head modelled in relief over the fireplace, greets the visitor as he enters the hall. The work is some of the best in the West of England, all that remains of a once more extensive scheme attributed to the Bristol craftsman, Thomas Stocking. The work of the upper floors, dated 1769, was shipped over to America in the 1920s, where it is rumoured to have gone to the collection of Randolph Hearst.

Painswick House (1735) is a Gibbsian essay possibly by the Bristol architect John Strahan for Charles Hyett, who had bought the estate in 1733. The core is a block of five by three bays. The south (present garden) front was the original entrance to a country villa known as 'Buenos Aires'. The ground floor has blocked rustication to the windows and alternate pediments. The attic storey has plainer Classical detail. The Greek Revival flanking pavilions, incorporating the entrance hall one end and a ballroom the other, were added (1828–32) for William Hyett by his brother-in-law, George Basevi, considerably aggrandising the house. The old entrance hall was converted with bookcases into a two-storey library,

Top left: *Stout's Hill, Uley. The house in Strawberry Hill style is attributed to William Halfpenny of Bristol, about 1750: this chimneypiece in the hall, with its trophies and extravagant Gothic elements, was possibly carved by William Paty.*

Above: *Alderley Grange, near Wotton-under-Edge, with its Serlian window, an elegant village Palladian house attributed to Thomas Paty of Bristol, c.1744.*

Opposite: *Poulton Manor, near Cirencester. Elegant restraint in this charming William and Mary village house: square plan with a hipped roof, cross-windows and central chimney.*

and there is Chinese wallpaper in the drawing room, offered for auction in a big sale of contents in the 1970s.

Painswick House is known today for its Rococo gardens, delineated in a series of views by Thomas Robbins in 1748. The garden was obliterated, planted with larches, and forgotten until the rediscovery of the paintings prompted research in the 1980s. Features include the Red House, alcove, walks, exedra, the Eagle House, a hermitage and kiosks, all of which have been restored, or reinstated piecemeal since then. The garden was opened to the public by the owner Lord Dickinson in 1984, and is now recognised as the best surviving Rococo garden in the country.

Castle Godwyn lies in Paradise, outside Painswick, near the site where one of Earl Godwin's battles was fought. It was called Paradise Farm, and rebuilt about the 1730s to the designs of a local builder-mason (Tim Mowl suggests one of the Bryan family) for William Townsend, a clothier from Steanbridge. The garden front has a segmental pediment with an *oeil-de-bœuf* window. There is a (later) central staircase, with a screen of arches to the balcony, one of many alterations of the early nineteenth and the early twentieth centuries.

Adlestrop Park, near Stow-on-the-Wold, is in antiquarian Gothic Revival style, built in two phases (1750–63) as a secondary seat of the Leigh family by Sanderson Miller, a gentleman-amateur architect, who had Gothicised his own house near Edgehill, in the Warwickshire Cotswolds. It has a cheerful Gothic Revival south-west façade (1759–63), with an excellent Gothic centrepiece, a wide gable with two-storeyed bay windows either side and Gothic glazing, beautifully ornamented with cusp-fretted balustrading and crockets, panelling and airy polygonal buttresses. The interiors today are unambitious and plain, and the Rococo gardens were swept away by Humphry Repton.

Stout's Hill, in Uley, is a fantasy in the lighter mood of Strawberry Hill Gothick, also about 1750, where the emotive sublime humorously subverts all Palladian-Classical restraint and correctness. The design is attributed to the Bristol mason, William Halfpenny, a prolific writer of architectural manuals and pattern books, including *Chinese and Gothic Architecture Properly Ornamented* (1752) and *Rural Architecture in the Gothic Taste* (1752), relevant here.

It has a castellated Gothic front, symmetrical, with canted bays, all the windows having octagonal glazing bars and ogee heads typical of Batty Langley's pattern books, a pleasing porch and an asymmetrical block to the north, terminating in a single projecting bay pavilion, like a turret. The interiors are also Gothic, including an octagonal staircase hall and a drawing room (contemporary with Paty's octagon room at

Badminton), whose chimneypiece has an overmantel of a bugle between turrets, possibly by William Paty.

Upton House (1752), outside Tetbury, is another elegant house, attributed by Marcus Binney to William Halfpenny. It has nothing of Gothic fantasy, and is a wonderful if provincial amalgam of restless Baroque details and dignified Palladian vernacular. It was built for Nathaniel Cripps, whose family had been settled on a small estate here since Elizabethan times. Its principal (east) front is stately and original, where everything is of outstanding quality and in ashlar, with seven bays and three storeys, under a balustrade. The attic storey has small windows, oval in the centre and segmental-headed in the wings. The first floor has Palladian windows with pilastered architraves, blind balustrading and pediments; and the ground floor is rusticated, all the windows with prominent Baroque keystones. The central three bays project slightly forward, where four, giant Ionic pilasters support a heavy pediment framing lavishly mantled, nonce armorials.

Towards the end of the century, the great Regency genius, Sir John Soane contributed no major works, but dabbled competently in the Cotswolds at Fairford Park, Williamstrip Park, which he remodelled with bowed wings in 1791, and Down Ampney House, to which he made alterations in 1799. James Wyatt remodelled and extended Newark Park (1790) as a Gothic Revival villa, described earlier. He rebuilt Lasborough Park (1794–95) in a Picturesque Castle style, with angle towers and machiolated parapets; it was remodelled later, probably by Vulliamy, for R. S. Holford of Westonbirt. Dodington (1796), however, is his most important and grand house in Picturesque Neo-Classical. Jeffry Wyatt worked at Lypiatt Park, adding a new east wing (c.1812) in a Picturesque Perpendicular, with castellated adornments. Lewis Wyatt modernised Estcourt Park in 1829–31.

Lodge Park, Gloucestershire

Lodge Park was built in 1634 for John Dutton (1598–1657), a wily, sociable and lusty Civil War politico, nicknamed 'Crump', after a cruel, disfiguring hunchback. He was a rakish gambler, dedicated to the sport of deer coursing, and one of the richest men in England. The Lodge was therefore built not to live in, or even to look on, but as a grandstand building from which to view the mile-long course, a gambling spectacle, which finished just beyond the Lodge. This was a race between sight hounds, like the modern greyhound, let after the terrified deer, which ran as a lure (like an electric hare) in front of the house, more or less where the road now runs. A painting, now in the Lodge, by George Lambert c.1740, shows the threefold arrangement of lodge, deer course and formal park.

Crump Dutton was acquiring land for his 'new park' from 1624 onwards, but it was subsequently landscaped to the designs of Charles Bridgeman c.1729 for his great-nephew, Sir John Dutton, Bt. The Lodge is mentioned as 'lately built' by Lieutenant Hammond, a passing traveller, in 1634, who was the first to note the resemblance to Inigo Jones's Banqueting House in Whitehall.

The Lodge is a Classical ensemble in a simplified Inigo Jones manner, the most progressive building of its date in the Cotswolds. *Country Life*'s Clive Aslet describes the energy of the design: 'bursting with architecture.' Like the gatehouse at Stanway, it was long attributed to Jones himself, and that may

Above: *The east front, the perfect Palladian grandstand building once attributed to Inigo Jones, is progressive for its date (before 1634) in the Cotswolds.*

Right: *A portico with a balustrade stands in front to form the viewing platform; the quirky miniature arcading of the balustrade echoes the rusticated loggia below.*

be why Lord Burlington commissioned a drawing by Henry Flitcroft about 1750 (though he records a purer, 'corrected' version), and then why it survived the depravations of the nineteenth century. The architect is unknown. It is putatively attributed to John Webb, or sometimes Sir Balthazar Gerbier, a virtuoso of a florid Netherlandish Baroque. A master mason such as Nicholas Stone is another candidate as executant.

The five-bay east entrance front is intact, with rusticated quoins and balustrading set around what would have been a flat roof. An arcaded loggia stands as a portico in front, with rusticated arches and parapet (it has scaled-down arcading), so that there are two levels of viewing platforms for a crowd of spectators. There are subtleties of detail, sometimes clumsily provincial and without Palladian precedent: shell-headed alcoves, and fenestration in cross-windows, with curious pediments, and crude busts sitting in the upper pediments; the balustrading is top-heavy, the chimney-stacks asymmetrical. These are features of the 'artisan mannerist' style, a loose jumble of quotations cribbed from Continental pattern books and the work of immigrant craftsmen. But the coarseness associated with the style is here restrained.

The elements of the plan are simple. The ground floor had an entrance hall and parlour behind, with a service room. Below was a substantial service basement (later infilled), the kitchen with two fireplaces, and ample cellars, equipped for Dutton's lavish and sometimes debauched entertaining, with wenching and gambling. A staircase tower provided access to the first floor, where a new stairway has been wonderfully copied from one at Cornbury, in Oxfordshire. The first floor in the main block consisted of one huge space, a 44ft banqueting chamber, apparently a double cube, with a central fireplace (now replaced to its original design, after a fireplace found in Sherborne House) and central windows, accessing a balcony in front from which to view the chase. There was a bedroom behind to the west. The flat roof above formed the main viewing platform.

The house fell victim to a succession of drastic internal alterations, each more radical than the last, until nothing of worth survived from the seventeenth-century interior. William Kent was the first to intervene, refurbishing the main house and Lodge about 1728, but his work has been obscured by later overlays. We know he designed furniture for the banqueting room, delivered in 1730. Whatever work he carried out was gutted (twice) in the nineteenth century, when new partitions were set up and a new range added at the back, replacing the original one to make it serve adequately as a dwelling, first for gamekeepers and ultimately as a dower house for Lady Sherborne.

Unfortunately, the interior was radically simplified again in 1938 by tenants, and again about 1960 by Charles Dutton, 7th Lord Sherborne, by which time it seemed to be architecturally ransacked. Sherborne House, the main house on the estate, was leased to J. G. Bennett, disciple, biographer and friend of Giurdjieff and Ouspensky, as 'a centre for adult education and creative transformation.' After Bennett's sudden death, it was sold and the house and stables turned ruthlessly into flats, when the interiors were obliterated for ever.

Lord Sherborne died without issue in 1982, leaving his Sherborne estate to the National Trust, and reserving the Lodge for the use of Betty Hall, his faithful housekeeper. The Trust commissioned a thorough archaeological survey of the building by Professor Warwick Rodwell. The interior of the Lodge is a scholarly reconstruction to as near as possible its original form, and was the first major project undertaken by the National Trust that relied on the interpretation of archaeological evidence. It was opened to the public in 2000.

Above: *The canopied chimneypiece dominating the great room on the first floor is a faithful copy of one found in Sherborne House, the main house of the estate. Furniture for the room was contributed by William Kent.*

Right: *The oak staircase is a careful reconstruction commissioned by the National Trust in the 1990s after one at Cornbury Park, in Oxfordshire.*

Badminton House, Gloucestershire

Badminton is a princely pile, vast in its massing and in its landscape setting, vaster. It is the grandest house in the Cotswolds, crowned with domes, the focus of the largest estate not only in the county, but reputedly in all southern England. James Lees-Milne said that one instinctively fumbles for one's passport in one's pocket as one approaches, as if negotiating the border of a sovereign state. It is the nearest the Cotswolds approach to a Palladian palace, set at the heart of its own mythic dominions, like a Central European *Residentz* among its estate villages and parkland. The coronets, the Tudor badge of the portcullis, the standard, with the lions of England quartered with the lilies of France, boast of a royal lineage.

The conception is more Baroque than Palladian. The parkland setting is intentionally formal, with its rides and radiating avenues extending the façades along axial vistas for miles into the countryside. The park isn't a hunting preserve, a pleasure garden, or an Arcadian wilderness which anchors the house to its landscape in the tradition of the Picturesque, but unambiguously a political statement of ducal might and potency. The main ride is terminated by Worcester Lodge, nearly three miles to the north, a soaring, magniloquent conception by William Kent.

The broadly Palladian house we have today is often attributed loosely to Kent. But in truth Kent only performed a poetic tidying and unifying, adding his touches of genius here and there. The architecture is unusually complex for a Classical house, its façades expressing the unwieldy restlessness of so much architectural tinkering.

Badminton shows a history of demolition, rebuilding, alteration and constant modernisation. Howard Colvin described it in his *Country Life* article as a great country house 'whose evolution has never been fully worked out', which remains the case today. Andor Gomme, writing in a *festschrift* for Colvin, sums it up as one of England's puzzle houses. At least six architects of national standing are recorded working in the quarter century from 1728 alone. The architectural history has only begun to be disentangled in recent years.

In 1612, Edward Somerset acquired the estate from Nicholas Boteler, whose family had been settled there since 1275. An early survey by Matthew Nelson of 1615, shows the

Elizabethan manor house where Edward's son Sir Thomas Somerset was the first of the family to settle, from 1617. It was little altered until inherited (sideways) by Henry, Lord Herbert, (later) 3rd Marquess of Worcester. After the Restoration of Charles II, he was raised to the dukedom of Beaufort in 1682 for his fidelity, and that of his father, to the Royalist cause, which had cost them dear. Badminton is largely his creation.

The Dukes of Beaufort had a royal descent from the Plantagenet kings in the male line, and reigned as Herberts, Somersets and Beauforts like feudal princes over vast areas of remote Wales. Following the destruction of their power base at Raglan Castle, Monmouthshire, in the Civil War, they were intent on establishing a ducal seat across the River Severn in the English kingdom. So the 1st Duke set about transforming the Botelers' manor house into the rambling palace of a magnate.

The core of the house remains the 1st Duke's Restoration building begun in the 1660s, flanked by tall towers, with (originally) five storeys to the U-plan fashionable at the time, with the old cloistered courtyard behind. The exterior was substantially complete by 166[9] – the date of a painting by Hendrick Dankerts – the interiors about twenty years later. The house may have been designed by John Webb (1611–1672), or one of his circle, with a centrepiece of flat

Top: *The east front. The centre section dates to the 1st Duke's house of the 1660s, with the attic storey and pediment added by Francis Smith in the 1730s. The pavilion extensions and detailing, such as the balustrades, were added by Wyatville c.1810, and the church was completely rebuilt in 1785.*

Above: *The west front from the Gibbs pavilion. It is largely by the 2nd Duke's surveyor, William Kelligrew, of 1708, with a later porch marking the everyday side entrance.*

central bays and Corinthian pilasters like the one at Webb's Old Somerset House in London (1662–63).

He incorporated fabric from the earlier building (whose windows can still be seen in the basements), and there are plenty of Jacobean gables on the early engravings. The present dining room contains the magnificent Grinling Gibbons carvings of 1682–83, removed here later from Beaufort House in Chelsea. There was an 'aviary gallery' in the main ducal enfilade to the east, where the great drawing room now stands. The north front remains the main statement: a sprawling block facing over the park, with a central dome and grandstand pavilions for watching the course.

The Duke also started to lay out the park on a gigantic scale, with thirty rides radiating from the house in a *patte d'oie*, while his Duchess laid out the privy gardens and parterres and hornbeam wilderness to the east of the house. The results are engraved in bird's-eye views by Leonard Knyff, about 1699. The neighbouring landowners entered into the spirit of their schemes, Roger North recording of them that 'divers gentlemen cut their trees and hedges to humour his vistos [sic], and some planted their hills in his line, for compliment, at their own charge.'

The 1st Duke died in 1699. The 2nd Duke, his grandson, had a short innings, adding to and improving the house and estate with his surveyor, William Kelligrew, a provincial architect of Bath. Kelligrew was responsible for re-styling the west front about 1708 as the everyday entrance (minus the attic, which was added by Francis Smith of Warwick). He added eyebrow window pediments to the north front, and built most of the estate houses in the village high street, all with his hallmark bolection-moulded architraves, including Essex House, now colour-washed a golden ochre.

The 3rd Duke, who inherited in 1714, re-styled the house fundamentally, transforming it from a Baroque palace into a Palladian country house, and completely updating the interiors in sympathy with Classical taste. He was an amateur architect, a man of parts, who travelled widely and left numerous designs in his own hand. He engaged the ubiquitous Francis Smith of Warwick as his architect, a flurry of whose bills are dated about 1732. Smith was responsible for the Palladian-style rustication of the lower floors and the fenestration to the north front. Inside, he decorated the great entrance hall, the most stately Palladian room in the Cotswolds, in which to hang the five magnificent pictures by John Wootton of the 3rd

The great hall was redecorated for the 3rd Duke by Francis Smith after 1732. The most sumptuous Palladian room in the Cotswolds, it has furnishings by Kent and five Wotton paintings, including the Arab Grey Barb *over the chimneypiece, and a Landseer on the easel. The game of badminton was first played here in 1863.*

PENINSULA
WATERLOO

Duke in various sporting guises, with his Arabian horse *Grey Barb* (1734), life size, over the fireplace.

After Smith's death in 1738, James Gibbs was commissioned to extend the wings and set about building the terminal pavilions, the great entrance archway proclaiming the forecourt, with massive blocked columns and pyramidal roofs. The interiors today are much as the 3rd Duke left them. Plans ground to a halt following his divorce from his Duchess, Frances, on the grounds of her adultery with Lord Talbot in 1744. The Duke died unexpectedly in 1746, leaving behind debts and uncompleted projects.

The 4th Duke, Charles, brother to the 3rd, was married to Elizabeth Berkeley of Stoke Gifford, near Bristol. An heiress and a bluestocking, she was the Cotswolds' first knowledgeable lady gardener and the great patroness and friend of the grotto maker Thomas Wright. William Kent was engaged and worked with his protégé Stephen Wright to improve the impact and coherence of the main façade, particularly the upper part, adding the distinctive domed cupolas in wood, so achieving, according to David Watkin, 'a perfect balance between the opposing tensions of Baroque and Palladian.' He erected on high a massive central pediment in double-decker form with lunette and gaping oculi, corrected the windows from Baroque to Palladian with faux wooden architraves, and (possibly) built on the rusticated entrance porch.

Kent's supreme achievement was the building of Worcester Lodge, which he never saw completed. Badminton's main façade faces north up the ride to this triumphal eye-catcher, three miles away, a bold and spectacular conception with dome, Serlian windows, quadrant lodges and pyramid-roofed pavilions.

The 6th Duke engaged Jeffry Wyatville to make extensions and erect the heavy parapets and urns on the main façade in 1807–11. He updated a number of the interiors in Regency

Above: *The library, with bookcases of 1733 and a Wyatville ceiling arranged in the 1st Duke's gallery of the east wing, forms a comfortable everyday sitting room.*

Left: *Dining-room chimneypiece by Francis Smith, with limewood carvings of 1682–83 by Grinling Gibbons, removed from Beaufort House in Chelsea.*

taste, notably in the formal rooms in the east wing, including the great drawing room and the library (ceiling), and rebuilt the top-lit great staircase.

Inside, the rooms are surprisingly domestic and approachable for such a palace of a house, with long corridors wandering through the service range to the west, and all the impedimenta of hunting and country life. The old kitchens, steward's room and servants' hall adapt well to contemporary uses. It is tantalising that hardly anything of the 1st Duke's Restoration house remains: the great ducal enfilade, with its state bedroom on the ground floor, the aviary gallery, the room all wainscoted with 'true East India japan'. Today, the main family rooms in the east range are of the Gibbs, Francis Smith and Kent generation (1729–45), with significant Wyatville overlay. The great hall remains the best room, where the game of Badminton was invented one dull winter's day in 1863.

The church was rebuilt as a Neo-Classical mausoleum for the Beaufort monuments (including masterpieces by J. M. Rysbrack and Grinling Gibbons) in 1782. The south front has declined to the back parts, with a François Goffinet garden (1990) but no proper façade. It is a jumble of corridor extensions and linking blocks added randomly to give communication to the early rooms, when the house was one room thick.

The gardens have been in a continuous state of creation for over three centuries. A long catalogue of great names has been involved. The 1st Duke's work was followed by George London, Henry Wise and Charles Bridgeman; then William Kent, Thomas Wright and Lancelot 'Capability' Brown in the 1760s. All have shaped the gardens, with the creation of an Italianate orange garden, a walled kitchen garden, numerous garden buildings, avenues, woodland walks, specimen trees and clumps.

The grounds have a wealth of later follies, eye-catcher barn fronts, *cottages ornés* and grottoes, deer houses, and a ragged castle. Some of these are wonders of frivolity by Thomas Wright, the Wizard of Durham, built c.1747. They include the Castle Barn (1748), two 'Gothick Slait Lodges', a hermit cell called the Temple of Uganda, thatched in 1747, and 'the finest surviving root house in England'.

The great Regency drawing room was altered by Wyatville in 1810–11, with plasterwork to Garter themes, chandeliers and a fine Neo-Classical Italian fireplace. The Badminton cabinet, now in Liechtenstein, is seen in the recess.

Dyrham Park, Gloucestershire

Dyrham is a special plan. The house is a formal masterpiece in the Anglo-Dutch style popular at the turn of the eighteenth century, an ensemble where house, contents, gardens, orangery and even stables achieve the quintessence of eclectic Baroque. The church stands shunted to one side, all that remains of the earlier medieval enclosure. Only the great gardens have vanished.

All seems to be confidently Classical, a striking counterpoint of themes interweaving elements of the Dutch of William and Mary (in the interiors), French style (west wing) and Italianate (east wing). But Dyrham is in reality two, or even three houses, arranged piecemeal in a sandwich. There are two façades. The long west façade is lower and proportionately longer, of full fifteen bays, facing downhill to the Vale. It is the earlier by nearly ten years, built in 1692. It is a pleasing if plain effort with delicate detail in the vernacular by a Huguenot, Samuel Hauduroy, member of a family of decorative painters and a second-rate architect, whose fee at £10 for the work was cheap.

The east façade, forming the entrance at the foot of the hill, is by William Talman, the 'ingenious' architect of Chatsworth, and dates to 1704. It is taller by a full attic storey, bolder and as grand as one of Rubens's palaces of Genoa. It is transitional but conservative, marking the end of early English Baroque. There are two, shallow, projecting wings, as on the west front, here enlivened with rustication, alternate pediments and a roof-line, according to Rudder (quoting the *Vitruvius Britannicus*), which is 'finished with a handsome cornice and balustrade, adorned with trophies and vases of excellent choice.' The heraldic eagle crowning the centre is by Harvey, the final touch in July 1704. Inside Talman's front are the state rooms, an enfilade in the French style prepared to receive Queen Anne, and the *piano nobile* above. The two wings are

Above: *The earlier west front in an urbane French Baroque style by Samuel Hauduroy, 1692–94, with shallow projecting wings. It has a balcony supported on scrolled consoles over the door, prominent balustraded parapet, and a central statue of Mercury, probably cast by John van Nost, the finishing touch of 1703.*

Right: *The jewel of the collection: the state bed in fringed velvet and sprigged satin, complete with its protective case curtains. It was made for the house about 1704.*

set back to back, and each is almost a house of its own. The large room in the middle represents the Tudor great hall of the earlier house on this site, of the Wynter family.

The Wynters were courtiers who had settled here in 1571, 'managers' of the Elizabethan navy machine, who had prospered selling timber in the Forest of Dean for its battleships. Members of the family included John Wynter, who was Drake's Vice-Admiral and second in command when he circumnavigated the globe in 1578. John's nephew was Sir William Wynter, Vice Admiral of England and Master of Naval Ordnance, who played a prominent role in the defeat of the Armada. In 1686, their descendant Mary Wynter married William Blathwayt (?1649–1717), an ambitious London barrister and diplomat in the The Hague.

By then he was Secretary at War and rose to become Secretary of State to William III during the wars in France and Flanders. He was subsequently an administrator of the thirteen colonies of North America. John Evelyn commended him as 'very dexterous in business' and as one who had 'raised himself by his industry from very moderate circumstances.' As he rose at court, he seized the opportunities to prosper by every means available to him – salaries and sinecures, bribes, emoluments and embezzlements and appointments – and founded the family's fortune. The house rose as his riches multiplied, with additions and constant improvements. He was sly, ruthless, and mean in paying his bills, and often absent on state business, resulting in good documentation of building work. He sat as a Whig MP for Bath for seventeen years. In his favour, he was cultivated in the arts of music and architecture. His wife Mary died young, and by 1691 he had come into the estate and without much effort founded a dynasty. He went on to build the house as a widower, smugly, to express the consolidation of his success.

The house he built shelters in a deep combe under the Cotswold edge, approached along a twisting drive from the

Above: *The rich interior schemes survive remarkably complete from Blathwayt's time, furnished in the Anglo-Dutch style of the late seventeenth century. The walls in this ante-room are hung with Mortlake or Soho tapestries illustrating the story of Diogenes and Alexander (left).*

Right: *The great hall, on the site of its Tudor predecessor, showing the chimneypiece where a dummy board figure of a servant is propped up as a fire screen. The panelling is grained to resemble cedar.*

Bath road on the top of the hill. (The original entrance was from below, to the west.) There is parkland stocked with deer along the landscaped approach now framing the house, which appears on a level platform hollowed out in the dip below.

In the eighteenth century the gardens were considered the most remarkable feature. Formal water gardens in the Dutch style were reinvented for a hillside site, perhaps unique in England. George London was called in to advise. There was ample water from limestone springs. The gardens descending in terraces are illustrated in the Kip engraving of 1712, with a fountain by Claude David of Neptune from which water cascaded 224 steps down the hillside to be ducted under the stables to a canal, or 'mill pond', on the west side of the house. Water features and parterres of the Baroque sprawled both sides of the house, requiring prodigious levelling to establish and more prodigious labour to maintain. There were three canals, two cataracts, a wilderness, pavilions, and four or five fountains. By 1779, the 'curious water garden' is described as 'much neglected and going to decay.' Such gardens had in any case become unfashionable, and all this was swept away by George Repton and others in the years after 1800 to create the English landscape garden we see today.

William Blathwayt lost out as a Whig under the Hanoverian succession and retired to Dyrham in 1710, where he remained for the last seven years of his life. His descendants could never match the fortune that he had accumulated, and apart from updates to the family rooms, creating the present drawing room and dining room in the early nineteenth century, little has been altered. Much of Blathwayt's collection remains. Two contemporary inventories survive to indicate the arrangement and furnishings of the rooms in his day, mentioning Japan Closets and Clouded Rooms.

The interiors are strikingly Dutch, in the taste of the last decade of the seventeenth century exemplified by Daniel Marot and interiors in Hampton Court, Chatsworth and Ham House. The Baroque planning is unusual, with the house laid out in apartments of three to six rooms *en filade*. There are two entrance halls west and east, and two staircases, the 'best staircase' (east wing) in cedar wood full height, the west one in walnut. The great room on the east front with marble fireplaces is closed to the public.

Dyrham was acquired by the National Heritage Memorial Fund from Justin Blathwayt in 1956, and the National Trust took it over later that year.

Above: *The earlier west front – the original entrance front – of 1692 is long and low, with close fenestration and Italianate double stairway to the terrace, by a little-known Huguenot, Samuel Hauduroy. Projecting pavilion wings enclose a* cour d'honneur *in the French style. The church alone survives from the medieval arrangement.*

Cirencester House, Gloucestershire

Cirencester House has always been considered rather a plain house set in Elysium. Even Allen Bathurst, the 1st Lord Bathurst (1684–1775), who created it as his own architect in 1715–18, lamented the shortcomings of his new seat, questioning his friend and collaborator, the poetic genius Alexander Pope, 'how it comes to be so oddly bad.' After his Tory party fell from favour on the death of Queen Anne in 1714, he retired aged thirty from political life and devoted his considerable intellect and energy to his garden. He had a long life and strong will, and his plans were still being followed through all the changes in fashion by his heirs into the nineteenth century. It is therefore the most complete example of the English landscape garden, and arguably the best.

Allen Bathurst inherited on the death of his father, Sir Benjamin (who had bought the estate nine years earlier), in 1704. In 1705, at the age of twenty-one, he was elected MP for Cirencester, and by 1712 he was raised to the peerage in order to swamp the House of Lords with a voting majority to force through the controversial Treaty of Utrecht.

The house or 'Mansion' at Cirencester is set on the western edge of the town centre, concealed behind an immense three-quarter circle of yews, a battered hedge, 30 foot tall and always impeccably trimmed, which enfolds the entrance courtyard under its cloak. A great rusticated and vermiculated gateway whose door seems ever closed, marks the axial

Above: *The avenue, with its axis on the church, dominates the great landscape garden laid out by Allen, the 1st Earl Bathurst. His friend, the poet, Alexander Pope pronounced his woods 'the finest in England'.*

Right: *The east entrance front behind the yew hedge faces the town. The plain façade was probably designed by the 1st Earl about 1715–18, with remodelling by Robert Smirke about 1830.*

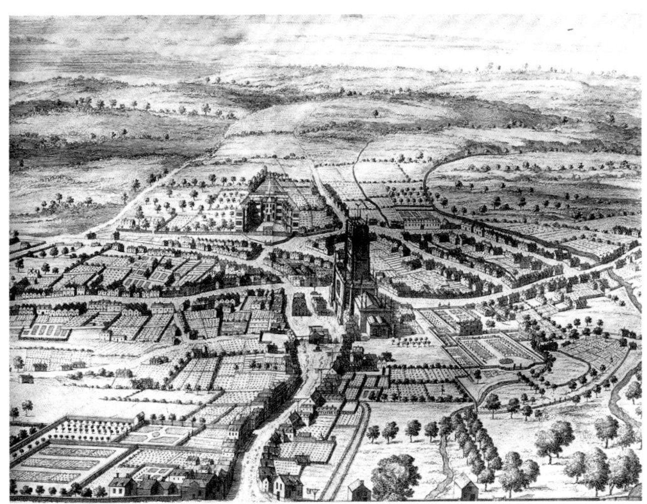

entrance to the town. The house stands (probably) on the site of Cirencester Castle, replacing a U-plan house called Oakley Grove built for Sir John Danvers in the late sixteenth century.

The east façade behind the hedge is a plain block, tall, thin and almost without ornament. It may follow the foundation of the old Elizabethan house, so the rooms were narrow in proportion for Georgian ornament. It was built by an Oxford master mason, William Townsend. It was altered for the 3rd Earl about 1830 by Sir Robert Smirke, bringing the ground floor of the east front forwards into the forecourt in order to make the rooms broader within. Smirke had already added a service block to the north. The most integral façade is the one to the west, facing over the park.

The park is the greatest achievement of the 1st Lord Bathurst. In 1716, he acquired the Sapperton estate of the Atkyns family to the west, with 10,000 acres of Oakley Wood, and proceeded to pull down an acceptable Jacobean manor house. In 1718, he called in the advice of the poet and gardener, Alexander Pope, to conjour the 'twilight groves and dusky caves' of the Longinian sublime and help him plan the landscape park with the 'amiable Simplicity of unadorned Nature.' Pope rose to the challenge, and would visit for months at a time, staying in follies in the park if necessary, and becoming devoted to the noble Bathurst, whose friendship and patronage, he later declared, animated his youth. The landscape began to take shape as an enchanted forest, where Pope, writing to Robert Digby (in May or June 1722) described himself as 'the magician appropriated to the place, without whom no mortal can penetrate into the recesses of those sacred shades.'

In 1721, Bathurst started building a wood house in 'the Elysian groves of Cirencester', which evolved with Pope's help into the building called successively the 'Hermitage in the Wood', 'King Arthur's Castle' and finally 'Alfred's Hall'. It is now taken to be the earliest recorded Gothic garden building in England, incorporating fragments of Sapperton Manor.

Bathurst was 'the vivacious earl' who with Pope's help over a period of sixty years laid out a miraculous conception of rides and walks among the extensive woodland, with temples and forts and seats, a statue of Queen Anne raised on a pillar on the avenue from the house, obelisks marking ancient fragments from Roman Corinium, all worked into his scheme. The Broad Walk extends for nearly five miles from Cecily Hill to Sapperton, and is usually taken to be the longest avenue of trees in England. Pope's Seat (there are two seats there) is a Doric temple with niches, facing across a *rond point* of seven rides to Kemble Church. The Hexagon of 1736 stands near the house, to the north of the Broad Avenue, designed it seems by Bathurst himself and resembling the vivarium in the Borghese gardens in Rome. Ivy Lodge is a *ferme ornée*, half farmhouse and half farm buildings.

Cirencester House dominates the town of Cirencester, particularly the wide street of Cecily Hill aligned on the Broad Walk, and the former Museum of Roman Antiquities (built for Lord Bathurst in 1855), as well as the estate villages of Sapperton and Coates. Subsequent Earls became patrons of the Arts and Crafts movement when Ernest Gimson and the Barnsley brothers, Sidney and Ernest, settled at Pinbury Park on the estate in 1894.

Above (left): *Cirencester Park: bird's-eye view engraved by Johannes Kip for Sir Robert Atkyns's county history of* Glostershire, *published in 1712.*

(right): *Cirencester House from the tower of St John the Baptist Church, looking down the (former) elm avenue laid out by Allen, the 1st Earl Bathurst, after 1714.*

Left: *The narrow entrance hall as arranged by Smirke. The portrait of the Duke of Wellington on Copenhagen was presented by the sitter to the 3rd Earl and the Antique columns and busts were acquired by his son and heir, Lord Apsley, in 1814. Wellington had taken over the Bathurst town house at Apsley House, 'No.1 London', in 1807.*

Barnsley Park, Gloucestershire

Barnsley Park is the Cotswolds' most ambitious Baroque house. It lies behind a long wall in level parkland planted with beech, near Cirencester, on the edge of the Thames valley. It has all the drama and presence of the most articulate work associated with the dazzling intellectual circle which surrounded James Brydges, 1st Duke of Chandos, patron of the arts, Maecenas of Cannons (his house at Edgware, Middlesex, which was demolished in 1747). The owner of Barnsley, Brereton Bouchier, whose family had been settled here since the Reformation, married Catherine Brydges, the Duke's sister, in 1700. As a bachelor, he had first built Barnsley House in the village which bears the date 1697.

He may have begun his new house at Barnsley Park soon after, but the progress appears to have been halting, as if the plans evolved in the building. There was very likely a hiatus when Brereton Bouchier died in 1713, leaving an only daughter, Martha, who inherited as a minor, aged ten. In due course, she married Henry Perrot, MP for Oxford.

The dates on the rainwater hoppers and the entrance front are 1720 and 1721, though the archives show the interior decorations were being executed as late as 1731. The building of the house could span the ownership of the two generations, with a change of architect mid-stream. This would explain the clumsy external elevations, ill matched, with awkward transitions and top-heavy attics, and quirks of planning within.

Above: *The Regency west front was remodelled by John Nash for Sir James Musgrove, with the conservatory (since rebuilt), in 1806–13.*

Right: *The east entrance is attributed to John James, working in the 1720s. The exaggerated keystones, entablature and attics are bold English Baroque in the manner of James's colleague, Hawksmoor. It is reckoned the finest Baroque house in the Cotswolds.*

The house convincingly rises above its lack of obvious coherence; 'it is sheer architecture', wrote James Lees-Milne, nothing can be added, nothing taken away, like a teapot by de Lamerie. It is beautifully conceived and built, of rich golden ashlar quarried on the estate, comfortable and very grand. Yet the identity of the ingenious architect remains a mystery. There is little to go on, on stylistic grounds. Christopher Hussey attributed Barnsley to John Price of Richmond, the fourth architect at Cannons. And it is true that Price's designs for Cannons resemble the completed work at Barnsley.

Gervase Jackson-Stops preferred Sir James Thornhill, painter and muralist, as the architect. It is unmistakably his bust in the hall (not Raphael's) with that of Palladio. Bigland in 1791 comments on the best masters completing a decorative scheme in the saloon with frescoes, no longer surviving. Thornhill had the competence, practising architecture, according to one contemporary, '*comme un homme de métier.*'

David Verey, the architectural historian who lived at Barnsley, followed by Alan Brooks, suggested a more complicated sequence of collaboration: John James (connected with Twickenham), possibly reworking earlier plans he had to hand by William Talman, the architect of Dyrham's west front (and the architect at Cannons who preceded James). James was the architect of St George's, Hanover Square, and Hawksmoor's colleague, a student of Continental architectural practice, and translator of key contemporary texts on architecture, gardening and decoration; but he rarely rises above dullness as a designer.

Barnsley exudes a luxuriant graciousness, yet the house yields; it is somehow not as overpowering as it looks. The drive approaches the east entrance front through parkland, revealing splendid façades, sometimes attributed to Hawksmoor himself. The east front has nine bays, the three central ones breaking forward with forceful emphasis like a temple, and there are giant Corinthian pilasters to the centrepiece with a heavy entablature and a central pediment of Baroque exaggeration. The ground floor windows have heavy keystones, some in triplicate, recalling a conceit of Vanbrugh.

The south front is recessed between projecting end bays, forming useful dressing rooms at the angles. The Corinthian pilasters are here carried boldly across the façade. The east front is by John Nash, responsible for a final updating in 1806–10 for Sir James Musgrave, Bt. He may have altered it with its bowed centre when he worked here, fitting out the library in Empire style, and adding a conservatory (rebuilt c.1989), which sits a little uneasily with the early Georgian ensemble, and the pepper pot lodge.

Inside, there is superb decoration to match. The glory of the house is its two-storey hall, with magnificent stucco plasterwork. 'The ceilings are done by the best Italian masters', according to Samuel Rudder writing in 1779. They are indeed lavish and lovely, and usually attributed to Artari and Bagutti, though Christopher Hussey favoured Charles Stanley as the craftsman.

The ceiling with rosettes framed in the coving is in the manner of Gibbs, where Venus and Cupid frolic in the centre, and philosophers stare stoically from their socles, set sombrely below Plenty and Wisdom and the Elements in the attic above. The hallway leads through three arched openings into an inner hall, also full height, where there is more plasterwork, with busts in the niches and a foison of plaster fruits and flowers like Grinling Gibbons. Medallions continue up the stairwell and there is an overmantel to the chimneypiece in the panelled oak room on the first floor.

Two spinster daughters of Henry and Martha Perrot lived on to 1778, when a distant relation, Sir James Musgrave inherited, aged twenty-one. He commissioned work to the dining room by Anthony Keck and to the library by Nash. He died in 1814, and the house stayed in the Musgrave and then Wykeham-Musgrave families for another 120 years.

Lady Violet Henderson bought Barnsley in 1934, and on her death, it passed to her son, the 2nd Lord Faringdon. He restored the house and laid out the formal garden, then in 1963 sold to his nephew, later the 3rd Lord Faringdon. He planted thousands of beech trees and in the early twenty-first century gave over the house to his second son, Thomas Henderson.

Above: *The Nash library is fitted out in English Empire style.*

Right: *The two-storey entrance hall is a triumph, with Italian stucco plasterwork attributed to Artari and Bagutti, c.1731.*

Nether Lypiatt Manor, Gloucestershire

Nether Lypiatt is the stately home in miniature, with a striking symmetry. It is the understated perfection of a static retro-Classicism. Here is everything of the conservative post-Restoration house in the manner of Coleshill (burnt down in 1952) and Ashbourne House, both in Berkshire, or in the Cotswolds of Fairford Park (demolished). But here it is reproduced feelingly, often compared to a doll's house, approachable and intimate. It is eminently covetable; we can imagine living here, perhaps, enchanted by its seductive harmonies, and several connoisseurs of houses have pronounced it to be their favourite house in England.

The façades are just 46-foot wide, and of a stately height emphasised by soaring chimneys, suggesting a cube. Palatial magnificence is distilled to the scale of the *gentil'hommière*, both without and within. The flanking pavilions give a sense of stability, though the north-west one was only added by Percy Morley Horder in 1931.

Gate piers and wrought iron railings screen the house from the lane. A vision in grey stone, 'the colour of a guinea-fowl's plumage' (wrote Osbert Sitwell) looms above. There are four storeys. A basement and cellar allow for a Cotswold version of a *piano nobile*, approached up steps from the front. Inside, the plan is compact, a miracle of contrivance, with the stairway converting to an open well as it ascends, simple wainscot panelling and bolection-moulded chimneypieces, a dining room with a balcony giving over the falling ground of the valley beyond, and bedrooms arranged as scaled-down apartments, en suite with dressing rooms and closets.

The house was built for Judge Charles Coxe, a local MP for Cirencester and later Gloucester, said to be a hanging judge, who inherited in 1699. Work could have started soon after, though the hopper heads carry his cipher, a crowing cock, and

Above: *The south front emphasises the compact plan of 46-foot square; the dormers squeeze uncomfortably between the chimneys.*

Left: *The west entrance front seen through the gate piers is perfection in miniature, c.1715. Stairs lead up to a scaled-down* piano nobile.

the date, 1717. Puzzlingly, it is mentioned as 'a very neat, new-built house' by Sir Robert Atkyns five years earlier.

A stone obelisk in a dingle south of the grounds commemorates the Judge's faithful horse whose spectre is supposed to haunt the place, to a clatter of hoofs heard on Christmas Eve. The plaque which honoured his name was stolen sometime before 1934:

My name is Wag that rolled the green,
The oldest horse that ever was seen.
My years they number forty-two,
I served my master just and true.

Nether Lypiatt stayed in the family of Judge Coxe's descendants until 1884, when it was sold off from the Rodmarton estate by Michael Biddulph. The house remained unaltered and unlived in, until Corbert Woodall bought it in 1914 and the architect Percy Morley Horder, a pupil of George Devey, started on a sensitive restoration, written up by Randal Phillips in *Country Life* in 1923. The articles apparently attracted the acquisitive curiosity of the exotic, passionate and

Above: *Violet Gordon Woodhouse, recitalist of genius, playing her Dolmetsch harpsichord.*

Left: *The staircase, with twisted balusters and wainscoting, broadens to an open well as it ascends through the house.*

Below: *The drawing room occupies the whole east front, here arranged with the Woodhouse early keyboard instruments in 1934.*

talented Violet Gordon-Woodhouse (1871–1948), née Gwynne, harpsichordist of genius and 'bigamist'.

She immediately bid for it and bought it with her husband, and lived here for the rest of her life. She lived together openly, devotedly and faithfully with four very different men in a *ménage à cinq*. They were Gordon Woodhouse, Violet's lawful wedded spouse, and the dashing Bill Barrington, later Lord Barrington. Two other admirers, the intellectual and witty barrister, Max Labouchère, and the musical First World War hero Denis Tollemache, had died by the time the Woodhouses moved to Lypiatt. Together they were known to a scandalised Society as the 'Woodhouse circus', until, her great-niece and biographer Jessica Douglas-Home writes, 'one by one, death separated them from each other.'

The next series of *Country Life* photographs published in May 1934 shows her decoration of the house 'which savoured of the eighteenth century', with stippled panelling, 'pieces of solid mahogany and well-worn chairs' (according to Osbert Sitwell), and Barrington portraits. Her collection of keyboard instruments – harpsichords, clavichords and virginals – dominates the main rooms.

Violet was a recitalist who became renowned as an interpreter of the repertoire of Bach, Purcell and Scarlatti performed on early instruments in her drawing rooms at Nether Lypiatt and at her house in Mount Street. Osbert Sitwell was a devotee and frequent visitor, referring to the house in *Noble Essences* (1945) as 'an old palace in miniature, as formal as a fugue by Bach, with its complex organisation to go with it.' She gathered a following of admirers who came to hear her play from all over the world, and her salon became a cult, filled with the great writers, artists and musicians of the day.

Her nephew John Gwynne inherited (briefly), praised by Violet for his 'spirituality mixed with great manliness', who lived into my own time. He became a Sufi adherent in his old age, with an ascetic Ghandian face, standing for hours on his head one day, or hunting in blue-and-buff with the Heythrop hounds the next.

It became one of the Cotswold's royal residences, if minorly so, when it was acquired by Their Royal Highnesses Prince and Princess Michael of Kent in 1980. The Royal couple formed an enormous dragon of yew topiary and planted a knot garden with the help of Alastair Martin, a garden of herbs and simples designed by Rosemary Verey, and thousands of roses, with a rose maze in front of the house.

Above: *The early-eighteenth-century sitting-room is panelled in beech.*

Right: *One of the beds upholstered in Queen Anne style. The Woodhouses assiduously hunted down antiques and appropriate furnishings.*

NINETEENTH CENTURY REVIVALS

The nineteenth century was predominantly the age of revivals, with restless efforts at renewal in the ancient languages of architectural history. The Cotswolds have outstanding examples of nearly all of the styles: Neo-Classical at Dodington and Wormington, Neo-Gothic at Woodchester, Neo-Elizabethan at Westonbirt, Neo-Tudor (Perpendicular) at Toddington, and Neo-Jacobean at Sherborne House (1829–34) and Campden House (1846), for Lord Gainsborough. The Anglo-Indian Arcadian at Sezincote is a one off, and perhaps most successful of all. For domestically many of these houses are overblown and unlovable, predicated on immense numbers of servants and broad acres, with a healthy rent roll to sustain them. Few of the larger ones remain occupied as family houses, though many have adapted well to new institutional or quasi-institutional uses.

Above: *Sezincote. A lone swan reflected in the lake below the long east entrance front. An exotic vision of pavilion Moghul architecture, with its stately onion dome, is set sublimely within the folds of an Arcadian valley on the edge of the Cotswolds. The architect was S. P. Cockerell, c.1810.*

Left: *Westonbirt, near Tetbury, with the garden entrance in the angle: a riot of historical styles from Jacobethan and Flemish to Loire Renaissance, and on a palatial scale, by Lewis Vulliamy, 1864–74.*

The earlier nineteenth-century houses were often rebuildings in the latest style by the old landed families on their estates, sometimes on new sites. By the mid-century, there were increasing numbers of predominantly merchant houses, as new money poured in from the Empire, and the new rich wanted to express their wealth and status in grand houses.

Kingsley and Hill in *The Country Houses of Gloucestershire 1830–2000* note a peak of building activity about 1865, after a period of slowly increasing prosperity. Agricultural rents saw a decline in the 1880s, and then rapidly recovered with feverous activity in the decade leading up to the First World War, while after the War new projects bounced back pretty quickly.

There are several essays in Italianate of the High Victorian period. Cowley Manor is a textbook example in the Italianate of 1855–57 by Sir Charles Barry's pupil and assistant, the competent George Somers Clarke, but it was enlarged rather tastelessly forty years later with colonnades for Sir James Horlick, the malted milk king. Tortworth Park (under the edge of the Cotswolds, of 1849–53) and Owlpen House (built 1848; demolished 1956) are both early works by Samuel Sanders Teulon. Rendcomb House, near Cirencester, was built for the Jewish bullion broker Sir Francis Henry Goldschmid in conventional Italianate of 1867, but more successful are the French Renaissance stables with steep roofs and sumptuous Baroque lucarnes in the 'Rothschild' manner. Colesbourne Park (1853–55) was built for Henry Elwes by David Brandon in heavy Jacobean, but a soft Bath stone was chosen, which crumbled away in decades, and it was replaced with a design in reconstituted stone in a simplified Jacobean in 1958–60. Today it has one of the best snowdrop gardens in the country, and a fine collection of over 200 rare trees.

Some of the best specimen plantings are at Batsford Park and Westonbirt, set in landscapes Japanese or English, with their important arboretums. These are exceptional among Victorian houses for being noticed in the early volumes of *Country Life*. Others were too close to its own time to be assessed in the critical literature of the country house.

Variants of Gothic are exemplified at Quarwood (1866–69), near Stow-on-the-Wold, by J. L. Pearson, now altered beyond recognition, and Beaudesert Park (1871–73), near Minchinhampton (originally called Highlands), by Ewan Christian, designed in a Midland timbered style after the 'Old English' of George Devey.

Notable additions to houses of the Georgian period include the flanking wings (1828) at Painswick House, added by George Basevi, brother-in-law of the owner W. H. Hyett, and large wings (1873) at Barrington Park by J. M. Anderson. Basevi also worked at Gatcombe Park in the 1820s, adding stables and a curved conservatory for David Ricardo. Adaptations include Sudeley Castle and Lypiatt Park.

Angeston Grange in Uley is the Cotswolds' only *cottage orné*, built for the clothier, Nathaniel Lloyd, owner of a mill in Cam, sometime after 1811. It follows the style of the cottage orné inflated to the scale of a country house, to a precedent popularised with the completion of the Duke of Bedford's Endsleigh Cottage (begun in 1810) in Devon by Sir Jeffry Wyatville, and more locally John Nash's project of rustic cottages in village Picturesque at Blaise Hamlet, outside Bristol.

It has a long irregular façade, with hipped gables, extravagant (altered) barge-boards and the vertical thrust of chimneys, balanced by a horizontal verandah. Inside, there are conventional late-Georgian reception rooms, altered several times since they were built.

The core of Wormington Grange, near Broadway, is attributed to the local architect Anthony Keck, with two extravagant bow windows, full height, to the south. In 1826–28, it was doubled (at least) in size by Henry Hakewill (1771–1830) in a carefully executed Neo-Greek style for Josiah Gist. He added an imposing entrance façade to the east in fine ashlar, based on the (destroyed) Temple of Ilissus in Athens, drawn by James Stuart in the 1750s. A central pedimented porch with Ionic pillars has projecting bays either side, with panelled pilasters, and long tripartite windows above. It is the best Neo-Greek house in the North Cotswolds, completed with a fine top-lit staircase inside.

Above: *Wormington Grange, near Broadway. The south front, with two full-height bay windows, attributed to local architect Anthony Keck in the 1770s.*

Right: *Angeston Grange, at Uley. The south front of this* cottage orné *in a striking orange-ochre limewash.*

Sezincote House, Gloucestershire

Sezincote stands like a dream of Kublai Khan on the eastern edge of the Cotswolds, with its stately onion domes of pleasure. The exotic pavilion architecture of India dominates a Picturesque landscape of the English countryside, out of key, presenting an ambiguous translocation from East to West.

But Sezincote's dream is rooted in memory and history, a personal evocation of the travels and architectural reminiscences of its builders. The circle included the Cockerells, the owners; Thomas and William Daniell, the willing artist begetters; and Warren Hastings, the nabob of nabobs who had settled a few miles away at Daylesford.

In 1795, Colonel John Pepys Cockerell, descended from a nephew of the diarist, bought the estate, having made his pile in India through various employments with the East India Company. But he died soon after, in 1798, when his youngest brother Charles inherited (later a baronet and MP for Evesham), employing in turn another brother, Samuel Pepys Cockerell, as architect for a new house in the Indian style. He had been a Surveyor to the East India Company, and had already designed Daylesford House (1788–98) for Warren Hastings, the first Governor General of Bengal.

Their architectural fantasy was developed under the inspiration of the topographical artists Thomas and William Daniell, who had travelled throughout the sub-Continent 1786–93, observing, noting, and producing hundreds of watercolours of landscapes, buildings and architectural features, with a concern for accuracy symbolised by their use of the *camera obscura*. They published their series of lithographs of *Oriental Scenery* in six volumes in 1808.

Above: *Onion finials form a cresting to the roof looking east down the valley.*

Left: The trompe-l'œil *murals to the dining room, an enchanting capriccio painted by George Oakes in 1982.*

Sezincote was built about 1810, as something new in Picturesque taste, and experimental, in saffron-coloured stone believed to be from Barrington. It translates a hoard of architectural details energised with Moghul references to create a mood of the Longinian Sublime. It is playful as the eighteenth-century Neo-Gothic or Neo-Greek had been; a fashion to succeed, even to surpass, the historicist experiments of Egyptomania, Chinoiserie, the Adamesque Pompeian; graceful, but with a hint of terror that we find in the Gothic novel, or William Beckford's *Vathek*. Such historicism was to continue through the nineteenth century till it exhausted itself in a return to native inspiration in the Arts and Crafts movement particularly successfully here in the Cotswolds.

But there is something more earnest and critical at Sezincote, creating not an idyllic harmony, but a sense of strangeness and tension in the romanticised, Picturesque landscape. Sezincote's architecture is couched in the calculated and artificial contrasts of the Picturesque style. In its dream setting, Sezincote is not just a scholarly imitation and paraphrase from little-known sources, a series of quotations of its elements of *iwans, chattris, chayas, jalis*. The Picturesque style relied on precisely this variety and unlikely combination of unusual elements to disturb and surprise the imagination.

Sezincote was built by the eighteenth-century generation steeped in the enlightenment legacy. They had learned from Orientalists like Sir William Jones that the Indian heritage, mythologies and Aryan languages derived from the same sources as the Classical civilisation of the west. The Cockerell brothers had settled in India and developed a sincere affection for its culture, and in retirement wanted to bring home some defining memory of place. Sezincote dates to the earlier Georgian colonial phase when there seems to have been a genuine respect for Oriental forms and culture in the European encounter with the East.

Outside, Sezincote imitates not a domestic building, but the mausoleum pavilions of the Emperor Akbar (1556–1605) and the later ornamented style of the Awadh rulers at Lucknow. The style is a deliberate mix of Muslim and Hindu elements of the subject peoples of the Emperors. The original pavilions were single storey, of course, and in their translation to the practicalities of English country house planning, a forceful horizontal emphasis is introduced to underplay the verticality of the three-storey fronts.

The south façade is the most gracious, with 'peacock tail' foliated arches from Rajasthan, and a central bay window, divided by pilasters with blind arcades. The copper-green

Sezincote from the south west with its eclectic decoration: Brahmin bulls and urns, peacock-tail arches, corner turrets derived from chattris, *and a cast-iron verandah beneath the central bay.*

onion dome is seen to its best effect here, raised above the chimneys, which had to be incorporated for the Cotswold winters. The main *piano nobile* hovers over a low storey, conflated as a semi-basement, hidden beneath a delicate cast-iron balcony, whose lattices imitate not Regency Cheltenham, but Indian *jali* work.

The façades are another picturesque play of contrasts, and do not repeat themselves. The long entrance façade is framed by pilasters and octagonal turrets at the corners, with lanterns like miniature pavilions, a diminished version of the Moghul *chattris*. The central accent is the *iwan*, the high portal niche of the Moghul style, with a hotch-potch of detail: blind arcades, scalloped niches to the window heads, Lucknow style, and humorous roundels in the form of Union Jacks high in the spandrels. (Pineapples abound, also un-Indian references.) Above, the attic servants' rooms are concealed, with tiny porthole oculi for windows, below an exaggerated eaves cornice, or *chujja*, overhanging on brackets. The windows of the main floor have eyebrow heads.

Its inner and outer worlds also show contrasting faces: outside Sezincote may play studiously with Moghul references, but the more private world encased within is European. The inner spirit is the confident Neo-Classical of the Regency, conventional and universal.

Inside, Sezincote is grand and Grecian, therefore, and the mood is a little later (c.1820). The house is entered from the long east front into a low basement, with family and service rooms, which sprawl generously at the back of the house. Two oil paintings by Thomas Daniell show his contemporary views of the house and garden. Humphry Repton seems to have enthused, encouraging the Prince of Wales to visit. He was so enchanted with what he saw that he immediately commissioned the Oriental theme for his Royal Pavilion at Brighton.

The central feature downstairs is a magnificent imperial staircase in cast iron, technically innovative, which rises in a

Left: *Contrasting styles of Sezincote: inside, the detail is Neo-Classical. The south-facing central saloon has grand coving in gilt trelliswork and swagged curtains by John Fowler depending from the eagle and lions' masks.*

Below: *The bed in the south-west room assembled from fragments of Sir Charles Cockerell's tented bed in the north pavilion, including the spears that supported a canopy.*

staircase hall to the main enfilade on the south side of the *piano nobile*. It is lit by two lunettes under the lantern dome, but all trace of this exotic feature is invisible here. A suite of dining room, central saloon and breakfast room gives on to the verandah, which overlooks the segmental orangery with its formal garden *à l'indienne*. The saloon has magnificent curtains by John Fowler depending in swags from a spread-eagle above the central canted bay window, and fine Anglo-Indian chairs, and a pair of commodes from St Petersburg. To the east are bedrooms with the best views, looking over the lake and the Vale of Evenlode into the Oxfordshire Cotswolds.

The Indian house is set in its eastern 'Hindu' garden, inspired by Thomas Daniell (and others). The drive from Bourton-on-the-Hill leads past Indian lodges over a conventional Palladian bridge, which has morphed into the Indian phantasmagoria, raised on eastern columns after those in the Elephanta caves. It is set with Brahmin bulls, weathered and worn, recast in bronze from Coade stone originals, dated 1814.

The bridge spans a streamside garden below, suggesting a gaping chasm. This is the so-called Thornery to the north, a narrow dell laid out with the sure artist's eye of Thomas Daniell. The Hindu sun goddess Sourya in Coade stone presides on her throne, standing in for Greek Apollo.

Cyril and Elizabeth Kleinwort bought the estate in 1944. The present Moghul paradise garden from 1965 was laid out with the advice of Graham Stuart Thomas. The house is now lived in by Sir Cyril's grandson, Edward Peake, and his wife, Camilla, and their young family.

Above: *The orangery extends like a scimitar arm, snuggling into the hillside. The end pavilion was conceived as an aviary. The cypresses to the Moghul paradise garden were planted by Graham Stuart Thomas after 1968.*

Right: *The octagonal north pavilion once housed the bedroom apartments of the owner, Sir Charles Cockerell.*

Dodington Park, Gloucestershire

Dodington is one of the last of the great Neo-Classical houses in England, grand and porticoed like a temple, with Corinthian columns. In style it is Classically eclectic, hovering somewhere between Roman and Greek, with Roman capitals and Greek proportions. There is a Picturesque counterpoint to the rigidity and earnestness of Neo-Classicism in the arrangements of façades, the relaxed, asymmetrical placing of conservatory and domed church, and the landscape setting itself.

It is a monument to wealth, built for a rich West Indian sugar planter, Christopher Bethel Codrington, on the profits of his estates (and, more horrifically, slave breeding and trading) in Barbuda and Antigua. The architect was James Wyatt, the date c.1810. Alexander Pope had admired the park around the old Tudor manor house, which stood on the site, for its 'situation romantic' in 1728. 'Capability' Brown landscaped it again in 1764, opening up the vistas, and providing two lakes and bridges, Gothic seats, aqueducts and a cascade building, and the drama of hanging beech woods. Wyatt, Adam's greatest and most successful rival, prepared his design in 1796 for a house commensurate with its setting, to a square plan set around the top-lit central stairway, of Imperial grandeur.

At the entrance of the mile-long drive from the Bath road there is a drum-shaped lodge like a Bramante *tempietto*, and an immaculate semicircular screen of railings, announcing the splendour yet to come. The entrance front of the great house in the valley below is dominated by a colossal portico, six

Above: *The broad hexastyle portico to the west front, Roman and Greek, like a temple: a search for a Neo-Classical version of the Picturesque by James Wyatt,* c.1810.

Left: *Inside, the entrance hall is sumptuously fitted out with columns of porphyry* scagliola, *compartment ceilings, gilded ornament, inlaid brass and marble floors.*

columns wide, beneath a Greek-style pediment, to form a *porte-cochère*, drawn (almost) from side to side across the façade.

Within, the interiors are just as impressive. There is plasterwork, *scagliola*, chimneypieces, doors in inlaid mahogany, gasoliers, columns galore – all supplied by the best masters – and Adamesque decorative schemes, with fine fittings to match. The entrance hall has screens with columns of porphyry *scagliola* at either end and, beyond the screens, a coved and coffered ceiling set with trophies. The crowning glory is the central staircase, lighter, and one of Wyatt's most majestic.The ironwork to the balustrades is earlier and more delicate: a Rococo creation of the 1760s removed from Fonthill Splendens, the house of another sugar magnate, Alderman Beckford, where Wyatt was working on a Gothick fantasy to replace it for 'England's wealthiest son', William Beckford. Over half the floor area is given over to staircases, landings, corridors and circulation space.

A wing with accommodation for sixty servants was demolished in 1932. Sir Simon Codrington (the 3rd Baronet of the second creation and a brother officer of my father's) broke up the estate 1980–84, and moved out with a few family heirlooms to a nearby bungalow, when Dodington was closed to the public.The house – which was said to have 51 bedrooms, 40 bathrooms and ten huge reception rooms – was 'hoovered up' in 2003 by the industrial inventor and vacuum cleaner mogul, James Dyson. He has erected a huge circular pool in the entrance court, reflecting Wyatt's noble portico.

Above: *From the south east, the austere Classical façades lack coherence: bow windows to the east, recessed columns in antis to the south.*

Right: *The top-lit great staircase with its Rococo ironwork of the 1760s is earlier than the house, having been 'appropriated' from Alderman Beckford's Fonthill Splendens, where Wyatt was also engaged.*

Westonbirt House, Gloucestershire

Westonbirt, near Tetbury, is the most ambitious nineteenth-century house in the Cotswolds, in a Jacobethan Revival style based on Wollaton Hall, by Robert Smythson, in Nottinghamshire. It was designed by Lewis Vulliamy after 1865, on the scale of a palace, to replace an adequate house near the site which had stood just forty years. He incorporated all the latest technology, of gas lighting, early central heating, hot water, ironwork. He also removed the village, and built for his client a London house, Dorchester House, in Park Lane, based on the Villa Farnesina, in Rome.

His client was Robert Stayner Holford (1808–1892), MP, whose family had lived at Westonbirt from 1665 and had risen from the squirearchy into the plutocracy through their stake in the New River Company, which provided London's water supply. He inherited the 1,000-acre estate from his father, who had pulled down the Elizabethan house, replaced it with a Neo-Tudor one in 1823, and first set out the arboretum to complement it in 1829.

The stonework everywhere is superb, excessive, luxuriant, and there are heavy-handed Mannerist references, Classical orders and unlikely juxtapositions of styles. The roofscape is a riot, which embraces French dormers, shaped gables, obelisks, ranks of octagonal chimneys, balustrades, and a tower decorated with strapwork under an ogival roof. Inside is the

Above: *The garden front from the south west with the orangery wing (to the left), in eclectic Jacobethan Revival of 1864–74, by Lewis Vulliamy: a statement of Victorian palatial for a plutocrat.*

Right: *Renaissance grand stairway with coffered ceiling. Westonbirt housed one of the finest art collections of its time until its sale in 1927.*

amazing full-height saloon, sky-lit with a gallery, leading to Renaissance reception halls, with sumptuous ceilings and architectural antiques, the most extravagant of which is the hall chimneypiece, incorporating elements of a Baroque altar. The great Holford collection of paintings, including five Rembrandts, decorated the rooms. Nothing of the period could have been richer, to the point of exhausting vulgarity.

Westonbirt has a virtually untouched Italian garden to the east, enclosed by two Neo-Jacobean gazebos by Henry Hamlen with fish-scale domes, which like the garden are earlier than the present house (1843). Other features, include a pergola, an orangery, a Pulhamite rockery and lake, and a giant conservatory.

Sir George Holford succeeded, and continued his father's tradition of opulence, maintaining 27 orchid houses and entertaining King Edward VII and then Queen Mary. But by 1927, Westonbirt was too large to live in or maintain. The incomparable picture collection was dispersed for £572,377 and the house became a girls' school, which has flourished since. Though the resident pupils, circumspect as to the architecture, claim the house would be a perfect location for a horror film.

Westonbirt is famous today for its arboretum, one of the best anywhere, originally 114 acres and now extending to 600 acres, which stands on the north side of the road, owned and managed since 1956 by the Forestry Commission and its successor bodies. The National Arboretum is open to the public.

Above: *The 'Italian' garden with ogival Neo-Jacobean and Moorish gazebos designed by Henry Hamlen in 1843 surviving from the earlier house and garden.*

Right: *Reflection of ranks of chimneys in the pool garden. The famous tree collection was started by R. S. Holford in 1829.*

Woodchester Park, Gloucestershire

Woodchester Park is the domestic masterpiece of the Gothic Revival, perhaps the most absolute of all Victorian country houses. Every element – the roofs and floors, the staircases, bath, gutters and downpipes – is built of stone of matchless quality, creating a learned anthology of neo-medieval craftsmanship. Its ideal is an uneasy anachronism, built four centuries after the Middle Ages, in the industrialised Stroud valleys, one of the first industrial landscapes in the world. It is an architectural anomaly, forcefully melding Northern French Gothic and Cotswold Tudor, and was long unknown and forgotten – until rescue came in the late twentieth century.

The house is set in the deep hollow of a medieval park, acquired by the Huntley family in 1564. Sir Robert Ducie bought the estate in 1631, and his successors built a Georgian house called Spring Park, more or less on the site of the present Woodchester Park, in the 1740s, which was later remodelled by J. A. Repton. The place was ready to receive George III by 1788.

In 1845, the estate was bought by William Leigh (1802–1873), from Little Aston Hall, Staffordshire, whose family had prospered in Liverpool merchanting and in land speculation in Australia. Leigh had converted to Catholicism under the Oxford Movement, and was intent on living a life of monastic austerity with his family, reclusive, pious and pure. He set about creating a house which expressed such ideals, and sought the advice of A. W. N. Pugin, the founding genius of the Gothic Revival. He recommended pulling down the old eighteenth-century house and prepared a design (which survives), but begged to bow out of the project. When Pugin died in 1852, Leigh transferred the commission to Charles Hansom, who had already built a monastery for Leigh at the eastern edge of the estate.

Above: *South front in Cotswold Tudor manorial. The Mansion, inhabited only by bats, lies brooding in a deep valley near Stroud.*

Right: *Gargoyle of a roaring beast. Everything is built of stone, down to the rainwater goods, and, inside, even the bathtub.*

About 1860, the project was taken over by Hansom's assistant, an unknown twenty-one-year-old enthusiast for the Gothic, named Benjamin Joseph Bucknall (1833–1895). He was the translator, friend and chief English disciple of Eugène Viollet-le-Duc, the French architect, restorer of medieval buildings, and theorist. Woodchester remains Bucknall's masterpiece, a powerful and original amalgam of his passions for the spirituality of French rational Gothic and the romance of Cotswold vernacular. The hieratic chapel is the *tour de force*, with a riot of Rayonnant late Gothic tracery to the rose window, tierceron vaulting, and an elevated squire's gallery. Everywhere Northern Gothic detail is deployed to demonstrate a system of building in stone, where the constructional principles are made manifest, carefully studied from originals: fan-vaulted ceilings to all the main rooms and corridors, bosses and buttresses, gargoyles in the form of fantastic attenuated leopards, ravens and owls. All is set round a crepuscular courtyard overlooked by a louvred clock-tower which soars above, with the date 1852, and the motto: *'In sapientia ambulate tempus redimentes'*.

Woodchester is one of the great unfinished symphonies of architectural history. For some unknown reason, the clock stopped and all work was suspended suddenly about 1868, the ladders and scaffolding and form-work left *in situ*. Bucknall retired young to Algeria, an exhausted genius. William Leigh, cursed by family deaths, had not the will, nor probably the means, to carry on. The building, inconvenient, impracticable, and eternally damp, was left a roofed shell, hollowed into the cold north slope of the hills. Only the drawing room, lierne-vaulted in stone with fifty bosses, was made ready for a visit by Cardinal Vaughan in 1894. For a hundred years Woodchester was lost hopelessly to history, abandoned, re-absorbed by its landscape, until it became the roosting place of bats and the stuff of local ghost legends.

The Leigh family held the estate until 1938, the year Evelyn Waugh gave a lecture there. The 'Mansion', as it was known by the villagers, survived, just, into the age of conservation. It was first described by David Verey, the local historian, who wrote in *Country Life* in 1969 that Woodchester is 'one of the greatest achievements of nineteenth-century domestic architecture in England'.

In 1989, the local council bought the house and then leased it to The Woodchester Mansion Trust, a buildings restoration trust whose aim was to restore the house to its 'profound state of abandonment'. The National Trust in 1994 acquired the environing parkland and 'lost' garden.

The approach from the south east, where the chapel is seen in the centre in Rayonnant French Gothic, with the clock tower behind.

THE ARTS AND CRAFTS MOVEMENT IN THE COTSWOLDS

The Cotswolds lay claim to some of the most important houses of the Arts and Crafts movement, and became the rural centre of the radical renewal in the decorative arts. The region was home, retreat or inspiration to a group of outstanding writers and artists, which included John Singer Sargent and Henry James, critics and poets, utopian architects and craftsmen living in village communities in Sapperton and Chipping Campden, and anarchist disciples of Tolstoy at the Whiteway Colony, near Stroud.

The Cotswolds came through the Industrial Revolution visually almost unscathed, because they remained a rural backwater. They lacked raw materials such as coal and iron,

Above: *Kelmscott Manor, near Lechlade. The Elizabethan east front from the garden door. William Morris loved this house as symbol and retreat: 'a place almost too beautiful to live in'.*

Left: *Eyford Park, near Stow-on-the-Wold, the rising terraces punctuated by the rhythm of the gateless piers designed by Guy Dawber, 1911–12.*

and were ill served by navigable rivers or the new infrastructure of turnpikes and canals; without these, the staple woollen cloth industry started to decline. Yet the Cotswold region by the late nineteenth century was becoming accessible to the national centres of artistic renewal in London, Oxford and the Midlands. Alan Powers suggests that 'one of the paradoxes introduced by the Arts and Crafts movement was that one of the most backward parts of the country was the right place to start a modern art movement.'

The elevation of the Cotswolds in the imagination from the 'ugly country' of William Cobbett in 1826 to the idyll of the late nineteenth century, glorying in the lyrical beauty of its limestone and landscape, is a direct result of the advocacy of William Morris (1834–1896). He arrived at the edge of the Cotswolds in 1871, when he and the Pre-Raphaelite painter, Dante Gabriel Rossetti, took a joint lease of Kelmscott Manor, a stone manor house set in the level meadows of the Thames, near Lechlade, as a summer retreat.

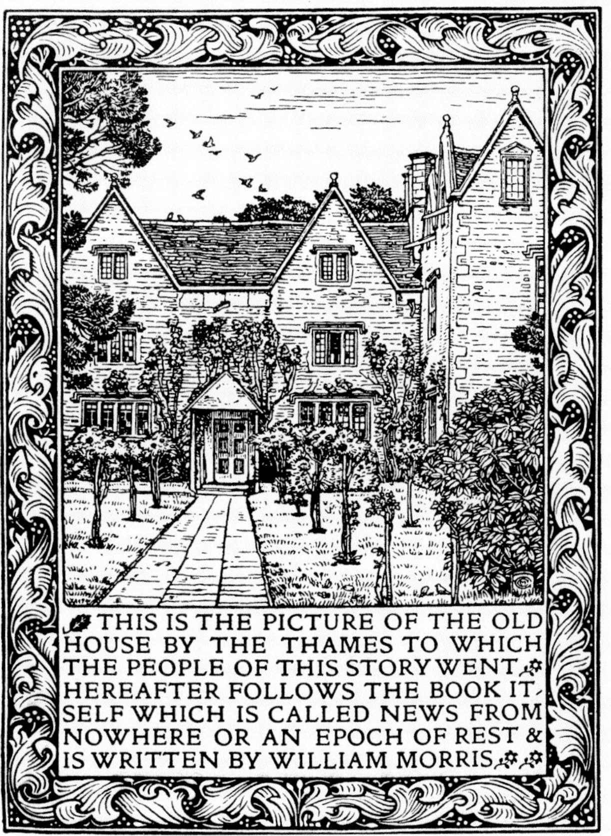

The best-known early project of Morris and his architect-collaborator, Philip Webb had been the Red House, near Bexleyheath, in Kent, in 1859. It is one of the defining buildings of the mid-century, radical in its simplicity and originality. The new 'homely' architecture recoiled from the falsification and degradation implicit in all industrial methods and the 'sham' of stylistic revivals; it was underscored by a revival of the domestic handicrafts and the collaborative processes that created them, from which 'The House Beautiful' could be resurrected.

Inspired by the social and moral commitment of William Morris (and John Ruskin), and the radical communitarianism of theorists like Edward Carpenter, in the next generation two concentrations of artistic settlement and activity developed in the Cotswolds: at Chipping Campden in the North Cotswolds, under C. R. Ashbee, and at Sapperton and Oakridge in the central Cotswolds, under Ernest Gimson and the Barnsley brothers.

Above: *Kelmscott Manor: frontispiece wood-engraving for Morris's Utopian romance,* News from Nowhere, *after a design by C. H. Gere, issued in 1893.*

Left: *Chipping Campden market hall interior. The wool village became a centre for the Arts and Crafts movement from the 1890s.*

It was not just the houses of the Cotswolds but also the villages which enthralled architects. Charles Robert Ashbee (1863–1942) was an architect, designer and romantic socialist. He founded the Guild of Handicrafts in 1888 at Essex House, Mile End Road, in the East End of London, developing its co-operative model and structure from the teachings of Morris and Ruskin, with the aim not only to set a high standard of craftsmanship, but also 'to protect the status of the craftsman'.

In 1902, Ashbee, a Pied Piper figure leading a 'joyous crowd' of seventy craftsmen and their families from the East End, settled in one of the North Cotswolds' most beautiful market towns: Chipping Campden. The Guild specialised most successfully in crafts, such as metalworking, enamelling and jewellery; Ashbee's interest lay in the book arts and he set up the Essex House Press as the successor to the Kelmscott Press, which had closed in 1897. The Guild was an idealistic venture, which went into liquidation in 1907, but it still has successors working in Chipping Campden today.

Ashbee worked on the adaptation of outstanding medieval houses for himself at Woolstaplers' Hall (1902–03), and the Norman Chapel at Broad Campden (remodelled in 1905–07) for his friend and collaborator at the Essex House Press, the Singhalese philosopher and art critic Ananda K. Coomaraswamy. This was Ashbee's major work in the area, bringing into domestic use a derelict Norman chapel with many early features, such as its prominent north and south doorways, and chancel arch. He created a music room and library in the old chapel and adjoining priest's house, and added a new service wing. Ashbee lived there from 1911 to 1919.

The late flowering of the Arts and Crafts movement in Chipping Campden is expressed in the work of the etcher, conservationist and architectural illustrator, F. L. Griggs, who settled in the town in 1903. He became involved with the sympathetic remodelling of several old houses in the village, and with his eye for detail also redesigned street signage and ironwork. He put into repair Dover's House, an early Georgian terraced house, where he lived from 1906 to 1930. He went on to build one of the most significant of all late Arts and Crafts houses, New Dover's House (mainly 1927–30), to fastidious standards of workmanship, nearly bankrupting himself in the process and testing the patience of his craftsmen and family, a project which he said became 'a sort of life's work for me'. Griggs founded with Norman Jewson and others the Campden Trust, an early conservation trust to protect the town and area, and initially Dover's Hill, from the threat of development.

The Arts and Crafts movement in the Cotswolds petered out after the First World War. Ernest Gimson had died aged fifty-four in 1919, and the Barnsley brothers died shortly after him, in 1925–26. As Sir George Trevelyan, a later follower, noted, Gimson died just as he was achieving widespread recognition and when his creative inspiration was at its highest: 'There is no knowing how great his influence on the Modern Movement might have been.'

Norman Jewson (1884–1975) was Ernest Gimson's foremost student and a pivotal link between the generations. Like Detmar Blow, he worked in collaboration with Gimson. He was younger than Blow and, surviving with a clear memory into his nineties, he was able to transmit in his friendships and his writings much of the lore and background of the Gimson school, and to carry first-hand knowledge of his design principles and working methods into the late twentieth century.

Jewson set up in practice on his own after Gimson's death and gained a reputation for the sympathetic conservation and remodelling of old buildings between the wars. He worked on houses great and small, including some ambitious manor houses, such as Aycote House, near Cirencester (1931), and major adaptations, such as Campden House, near Chipping Campden (1928–34). Apart from Rodmarton, he worked on the repair and adaptation of a number of houses, including Doughton Manor (1933), Southrop Manor (1932–39), Wormington Grange (1930s), Througham Court (1929), and Owlpen Manor (1925–26), his most notable work, and cottages at Kelmscott (1933). His last significant house was the little known Garden House in Westonbirt (1939–40) for Captain Guy Hanmer, in a whimsical, Classical vernacular, based on the William and Mary style, with hipped roofs and a Classical loggia with Tuscan columns. It has been recently altered.

Jewson was out of sympathy with Modernism, preferring (he would say) the puppets of William Simmonds, so beloved by Violet Gordon Woodhouse of Nether Lypiatt, for example, to the Muppets, which had appeared from America shortly before the end of his life. He ceased professional work in 1940, when the true country house tradition seems to have ground to a halt. We came to know him in his old age, a survivor and mentor, predecessor, and friend.

The influence of the Arts and Crafts movement was pervasive and penetrated deep into the subconscious of the local architecture of the Cotswolds. Through its philosophy of conservative repair the Arts and Crafts ideal continues to inform a careful and scholarly approach to the adaptation of many of the Cotswolds' old houses to the standards and conditions of the twenty-first century.

Above: *Chipping Campden market hall: Cotswold vernacular of 1627.*

Right: *Almshouses at Chipping Campden, built by Sir Baptist Hicks opposite his great house. They cost £1,000 in 1612.*

Kelmscott Manor, Oxfordshire

By the time he arrived in the Cotswold region, in 1871, William Morris had vindicated his youthful ambitions, and was firmly at the heart of the Arts and Crafts movement as a designer-craftsman, promoter, critic and creative writer. As a versatile designer of genius, he had transformed the decorative arts, including wallpaper and textile design, tapestry-weaving, furniture design, metalwork and stained glass manufacture, and taken them to new levels of expression. He developed the book arts of typography and fine printing with the foundation of the Kelmscott Press in 1891. As a theorist and critic he became an authoritative and energetic polemicist, a utopian and radical socialist campaigning for nothing less than the reformation of society through the arts in all their forms.

At Kelmscott, Morris spent his summers 'studying', he wrote, 'the [difficult] arts of enjoying life', discovering the surrounding countryside and its social history. In 1880 in his lecture, the 'Prospects of Architecture', he had singled out the average yeoman's cottage homes built three hundred years ago in the Cotswold villages (and not the 'distinctively Georgian ones') as being the ideal type of old English house. In his polemics, he defined an aesthetic that captivated a generation and helped shape that of *Country Life* in the 1890s. His later life and work at Kelmscott is described eloquently in the conclusion to his utopian novel, *News from Nowhere* (1890),

Above: *The Green Room hung in* Kennet *chintz, with Morris tiles in the fireplace.*

Left: *Kelmscott Manor, approach from the east, the main block of c.1570, with the high north wing (right) added about 1665. In this 'heaven on earth', William Morris spent his summers from 1871 to 1896.*

which he wrote amongst the grey gables and rook-haunted trees of Kelmscott with ' a sense of the place being almost too beautiful to live in.'

Over the following years, 'Topsy' Morris became a champion of the local vernacular architecture of the Cotswolds, from Inglesham Church to the cottage row at Bibury and the barn at Great Coxwell, 'the finest piece of architecture in England ... unapproachable in its dignity, as beautiful as a cathedral, yet with no ostentation of the builder's art.' He defined a new critique based on the study and careful repair of old buildings, their authentic textures and weathered surfaces, and pioneered with Webb the first conservationist philosophy with the foundation of the Society for the Protection of Ancient Buildings in 1877.

Morris's appreciation of the Cotswolds and his plea for its vernacular buildings enthused the early editors of *Country Life* magazine in the 1890s. Later, Christopher Hussey (in his article of 1 December 1934) saw Morris as the person who first directed attention to the austere poetry, the supreme if undemonstrative craftsmanship, of Cotswold architecture: 'With its definiteness of design and pleasing unity in colour and material with the *monotone* uplands, the architecture ... is a kind of domestic Touraine, the backbone of traditional English building.'

At the heart of Morris's vision was Kelmscott Manor itself which dates to about 1570, a gabled manor house of grey stone expressing generations of true craftsmanship which, with the Morris connection, made it an icon of the Arts and Crafts movement. Morris loved the harmony of the unaltered manor house in its Thameside setting passionately, admiring its 'quaint garrets amongst great timbers of the roof where of old times the tillers and herdsmen slept', and finding its stone walls and roof tiles so organically linked to the eternal geological substrates that it seemed to have 'grown up out of the soil.' Every traditional feature is relevant to the discovery of its beauty, the drystone walls, the graduated tiles of the roofs, which '[give] me the same sort of pleasure in their orderly beauty as a fish's scales or a bird's feather.' For twenty-five years, he filled the house with his life and energy, expressed by the textiles, ceramics and furniture to his designs, and that of his friends.

The entrance porch between two gables is approached between the standard roses of a small garden enclosed by stone walls – as illustrated on the title page of *News from Nowhere*. A high cross-wing of about 1665 looms to the

The white Panelled Room was the drawing room, with a chimneypiece of about 1665 decorated with swags and escutcheon bearing the arms of the Turner family. The armchairs are upholstered in Peacock and Dragon. *A painting by Pieter Breughel the Younger hangs over the fireplace.*

north-east corner, its double-gables projecting to the right of the entrance front, added across the central range. Two gabled towers rise with subtly battered walls. Mullioned windows in the attics have decorative pediments instead of hood moulds, and there are the traditional elm gutters.

Inside, the old screens' passage leads to the hall. Everywhere is Morris furniture and wallpaper, tapestries and textiles, many worked by his daughter, May Morris. There are William de Morgan tiles to Morris's designs, Mantegna engravings, seventeenth-century chimneypieces, with cartouches and garlands celebrating the arms of the Turner family, who had leased the house to him.

Throughout the village is evidence of the collaborative work of architect-craftsmen of the Arts and Crafts movement. Ernest Gimson designed the village hall and cottages, Norman Jewson further cottages, George Jack carved the relief of Morris set on a wall to a design by Philip Webb, who also contributed Morris's Viking-ridged tomb in the churchyard.

Morris's wife, Jane, bought Kelmscott in 1913 and furnished it with pieces from their London home, including her own embroideries, and with some Gothic furniture designed by Philip Webb for the Red House. The house was bequeathed to the University of Oxford by May Morris on her death in 1938; it subsequently passed to the Society of Antiquaries in 1962. Donald Insall restored Kelmscott Manor for them in 1968 and the house is opened regularly to the public.

Above: *The traditional village houses of Kelmscott, their gardens bounded with stones laid on edge in the local manner admired by Morris.*

Left: *Looking from the North Hall (before alterations of 1966) into the Panelled Room in the north wing.*

The Sapperton Group

Ernest Gimson (1864–1919) met Ernest Barnsley at the artist John Sedding's studio. United in their ideals, they decided to move out of London together with Sidney Barnsley (1865–1926), Ernest's younger brother. The three young architects sought a place to practise their ideals for the organic community and for the revival of the arts, and through them the reform of society itself. They settled finally at Sapperton on the Cirencester estate in 1894, and in due course became known as the Sapperton group.

Country Life's H. Avray Tipping was one of the first to recognise the significance of the Sapperton group in his essay on Daneway:

'Sapperton became the headquarters of a village industry directed by men deeply imbued with a love and understanding of ancient forms and ancient processes. Mr Ernest Barnsley, Mr Sidney Barnsley and Mr Ernest Gimson are among the leaders of a school that is seeking to create an original and living style in architecture and in the associated decorative arts, founded not on copying old forms, but on accepting old principles and evolving from them products which, while they retain a flavour of the past, are fully characteristic of the habits and aspirations of today. Mr Gimson more especially has organised and still directs the handicrafts which now give so much distinction to the little Sapperton community, and Daneway is available to him to use as a storehouse and showroom for some of the output ...'

Ernest Gimson was, like C. R. Ashbee, a generation younger than William Morris, and the son of Josiah Gimson, an engineer of the Vulcan Works in Leicester. He attended a lecture on 'Art and Socialism' at the Leicester Secular Society given by Morris in his home town when he was twenty, an event which changed the course of his life. Morris's insistence

that the way to reform the arts and society lay through a handicraft system for the production of furniture, textiles, ceramics, wallpaper, printed books, and above all for building itself 'made the profoundest impression on Gimson', according to the Arts and Crafts theorist, William Lethaby.

Gimson became the moving force behind the revival of the Arts and Crafts in the Cotswolds in the following decades, the genius behind the Cotswold school of furniture and design, described by Professor Nikolaus Pevsner in his influential study, *The Pioneers of Modern Design* (1949), as 'the greatest of the English architect craftsmen.'

Pinbury Park, near Cirencester, Gloucestershire

In 1893, Gimson and the Barnsley brothers moved to the Cotswolds 'to live near to nature.' They settled first at Ewen, but in 1894 they were offered a repairing lease, at £75 a year, of Pinbury Park, a fine Elizabethan house on the edge of Lord Bathurst's estate at Sapperton, where a group of barns and cottages cluster round the gabled manor house. It is set in an enchanting position above the beech hangers of the Frome valley, its garden planted with an avenue of yew trees known as the Nuns' Walk, after the nuns of Caen, who had owned the manor until the suppression of alien monasteries in 1415. The main block is a small T-plan manor house built for the Poole family in the late sixteenth century. It was altered with the insertion of panelling by Sir Robert Atkyns, the county historian of Gloucestershire.

Ernest Barnsley, the eldest of the three friends, occupied the main house with his young family, while Gimson and Sidney Barnsley converted the outbuildings for their use and occupation. Pinbury became the centre for the group's communitarian experiment, and they attempted to invigorate the old village life with vision and idealism, planning to found a utopian craft community.

Gimson began to lay down in collaboration with the Barnsley brothers the principles of the 'Sapperton' style in the years 1893 to 1900, defining a 'school of practical building', architecture with all the whims we usually call 'design' left

Above: *Interior of linking block at Upper Dorvel, with Gimson's delicate modelled plasterwork to the beams: 'simple as piecrust', 1902.*

Left: *Upper Dorvel, Sapperton, was Ernest Barnsley's house, formed by additions at either end of a pair of old cottages (in the centre), 1902.*

out. He described his role in a letter to the etcher F. L. Griggs with characteristic humility as that of a kind of 'King's carpenter', working in a medieval anonymous system. Philip Webb was a regular visitor to Pinbury, describing its craft community as 'a sort of vision of the New Jerusalem'.

When Lord Bathurst took Pinbury Park back for his own occupation in 1902–03, Ernest Barnsley was commissioned to add a library, inner hall and service accommodation. The library contains one of Gimson's best-known plasterwork designs, with trailing honeysuckle friezes, and ceiling beams with roses and monograms of Lord Bathurst. A fine stone fireplace is carved with a design of oak fronds, set with squirrels munching acorns. Bathurst offered to patronise the three men to build or convert houses for themselves in the village of Sapperton, using local materials and craftsmen.

Top: *Pinbury Park, near Cirencester, with rear wing rebuilt by Barnsley of 1902–03. Gimson and the Barnsleys had taken a repairing lease of the fine Elizabethan manor house in 1894, as the focus of a craft community.*

Above: *Pinbury Park. The dining room was altered by Ernest Barnsley, who also added a splendid library and inner hall for Lord Bathurst in 1902–03.*

Left: *The tall tower block at Upper Dorvel, on a sloping site: Cotswold vernacular revival, inspired by the high building at Daneway.*

Upper Dorvel House, Sapperton, Gloucestershire

Ernest Barnsley's house, Upper Dorvel House, is set charmingly in a dip to the north east of Sapperton churchyard. Today, it is the best preserved of the houses of the Sapperton group, formed by uniting two small cottages with a low linking hall set between them. At the north end, the cottage has been rebuilt as a tall, gabled tower block, inspired by the high building at Daneway. The south end is the kitchen range.

Inside it has some of Gimson's most inspiring plasterwork (c.1901). The low hall has a ceiling divided into four compartments with cross-beams cased in plaster; the designs evolve in refinement and density from the service to the parlour end, following precedents in vernacular tradition; there are little panels of flowers and simple friezes with trailing acorns, delicate in the play of the south light, only a few inches above head height.

The Leasowes, Sapperton, Gloucestershire

The houses which Gimson and the Barnsleys built for themselves in 1902–03 are some of the most successful examples of the late Arts and Crafts ideal on a cottage scale. Gimson's own house, The Leasowes, is built to a compact L-plan, with a typical Gimson stepped chimney and a roof that was originally thatched. It exemplifies the ideal of a haunting 'austere beauty': sparse and uncluttered, with plain whitewashed surfaces relieved only by the gentle play of light over the modelled plasterwork. We cannot imagine a Gimson house with wallpaper, or Neo-medieval conceits.

A new spirit of Modernism informed his work: the presentation of pared-down fundamentals, the concern with the honesty of structure and truth to materials, the exploitation of the levels of the site. But the emphasis on texture and tradition is quite un-modern: there are plain boarded doors with hand-made nails, stone floors, drystone retaining walls and steps. The organic quality of the modelling and contrasts of surface transitions are skilfully handled: random stone and the softness of thatch, the stark plasterwork. Henry Wilson, in 1899, described Gimson's architectural style as 'solid and lasting as the pyramids ... yet gracious and homelike.'

Right: *A pier terminating a drystone wall morphs magically into a dovecote at the Leasowes.*

Below: *The Leasowes, with its thatched roof (since burnt) and stepped chimney built by Ernest Gimson for himself, 1902. Compact, organic and timeless.*

Rodmarton Manor, Gloucestershire

Rodmarton Manor, near Cirencester, is the masterpiece of the Cotswold Arts and Crafts revival, a triumph of solid craftsmanship, on a much larger scale than the Sapperton cottages, epitomising the movement as artefact and symbol.

The medieval manor belonged to Gilbert, Bishop of Lisieux, at Domesday, and the manor house, known as Rodmarton Place, standing by the church had fallen into ruins by the time of Lysons' engraving in 1803. Claud Biddulph was the younger son of Michael Biddulph, a banker from Ledbury who had been left (by a descendant of the Coxes of Lypiatt) the Rodmarton portion of a large estate, which lacked a good house. In 1906, Claud Biddulph married Margaret Howard, who (according to John Rothenstein) became the driving force, reigning over the village like some great medieval abbess. Three years later they commissioned Ernest Barnsley to build them a new house on a level site, away from the village, to be called Rodmarton Manor. Progress was halted with the outbreak of the First World War, though it was substantially completed by about 1913 and ready for occupation by 1915.

While Sidney Barnsley and Ernest Gimson concentrated on furniture design and craftwork, following a blazing row about 1905, Ernest had maintained the focus of his interest in architecture. The work proceeded piecemeal, and slowly, to the value of £5,000 a year; out of income, of course. And true to its spirit, Rodmarton was a work of collaboration, of owner, architects, craftsmen, and villagers. It embodied noble philanthropy, providing work and instruction for the villagers and tenants, and an object lesson in self-improvement, truth to materials and radical craftsmanship. Supervision was continued after Ernest's death in 1925 by his brother Sidney Barnsley, who also designed much of the furniture, but Sidney died just nine months later.

The work was completed by Ernest's son-in-law, Norman Jewson, in 1928, who had already worked on the house before the War. Jewson's final work was the addition of the chapel with a cambered roof like an upturned cradle and a plain stone altar (1929), often described as one of the finest internal features of the house. He also contributed his characteristic ornamental leadwork, with hopper heads and brackets cast with owls, squirrels and rabbits. Many of the craftsmen too worked in this collaborative tradition, men trained from the estate who had worked with Gimson and the Barnsleys.

Above: *The long garden, with herbaceous borders between yew hedges and a stone wall, is aligned on Barnsley's summer house.*

Top: *The long north front to the plan of a broken octagon, with gables like the teeth of a saw, by Ernest Barnsley, 1909–13. The house was built in stages from the kitchen and family wings to the left (1909), and only completed with the chapel to the right (1929), using materials from the estate.*

Rodmarton was Ernest Barnsley's most important work. It is a swan song, which recapitulates the old traditional Cotswold style. It was 'probably', Jewson recalled, 'the last house of its size to be built in the old leisurely way, with all its timber grown from local woods, sawn on the pit and seasoned before use.' It was built entirely of local materials, by direct labour, from stone quarried on the estate, where the workshops were supervised by Alfred Wright. Despite the example of earnest moralism, the project could not anticipate the social dislocation which followed war, and failed to carry forward the ideals of tradition and the organic community. Instead both product and process became to the next generation an admirable curiosity, indulgent and whimsical, as the last of a long line of houses built by local craftsmen on the paternalistic landed estate, and ultimately a dead end.

There are subtleties in planning. The house develops along three sides of an octagon, one room and a long hallway thick, like an overgrown cottage, to a (shortened) butterfly plan. The entrance front is long and romantically asymmetrical, with a proliferation of gables, which *The Builder* described as resembling magnified saw teeth, set around a pool of lawn. The lawn suggests a village green, expressing the communitarian ideology. The house develops functionally from east to west, the architecture expressing accretive growth and the uses of the rooms within, developing the precepts of

Philip Webb and George Devey. First, the kitchen and offices to the left have steep gables on a reduced cottage scale. The next wing is taller, with three gables containing the nursery, family and garden rooms. The strong central block contained reception and public rooms, put to philanthropic uses. It has a prominent storeyed porch, with the date, 1926, and verses from Goldsmith's narrative poem, *The Deserted Village* (1770), cut over the door: 'Ill fares the land …' To the right is the final gable to be built, culminating in the chapel, still expressing a sense of feudal order, divinely appointed and eternal.

The two main façades stand in tension to one another, where the garden front to the south is grander, more formal, a straight block of three gabled bays, with a fanciful Italianate open belvedere. Inside are plain white walls, and raw textures of plenty of oak and stone, textiles and ceramics by Louise Powell, metalwork by Alfred Bucknell and Fred Baldwin, and panelling by Alfred Powell. There is a large hall in the centre, medieval style, now the library, which was opened for instruction in village handicrafts, for plays, musical evenings, meetings of the Women's Guild and puppet shows in a theatre contributed by William Simmonds. The bedrooms repeat the mood of calm and Spartan austerity, furnished of a piece. The roof timbers are exposed in the attics and passages, the rational but inventive functionalism of rafters and joists combining tradition with a hint of sparse Modernism to come.

The garden is closely integrated with the architecture of the house, a symbiosis of hard and soft landscaping, developing in complexity from a simple yew terrace in front of the house, with a long walk to the side, leading at the end of the axis to Ernest Barnsley's rustic garden house with a hipped roof. The sure hand of the architect is evident in the defining structure of walls, topiary and terraces. The planting was achieved by Margaret Biddulph and her gardener William Scrubey between the wars, fleshing out a romantic vision in the Arts and Crafts manner, which like the house manages to be liberal and squirearchical at the same time. A dedication over a side entrance commemorates the makers: '*A Wright Faber Tignarius/ W Scrubey Hortorum Cultor*'.

Above: *The hall arranged with uncomfortable benches for basketry and village craft activities*

Right (above): *The house is filled with an incomparable collection of furniture of the Gimson-Barnsley school.*

(below): *Bedroom with simple furniture of the Gimson school.*

Above: *The chapel was the last part of the house to be completed (1929); its austere beauty, with a subtly cambered ceiling, is typical of Norman Jewson, Ernest Barnsley's son-in-law.*

Right: *Upstairs corridor: the structural 'honesty' of the carpentry suggests Modernism, but skilfully reinterprets historical precedents.*

Above: *The chapel was the last part of the house to be completed (1929); its austere beauty, with a subtly cambered ceiling, is typical of Norman Jewson, Ernest Barnsley's son-in-law.*

Right: *Upstairs corridor: the structural 'honesty' of the carpentry suggests Modernism, but skilfully reinterprets historical precedents.*

Abbotswood, Gloucestershire

Sir Edwin Lutyens (1869–1944) is the outstanding name in Edwardian country house architecture, promoted by Edward Hudson of *Country Life* and employed by him at Lindisfarne Castle and Deanery Gardens – as well as for the *Country Life* headquarters building in London. By the early twentieth century, Lutyens was breaking away from the Arts and Crafts 'Old English' style towards a simplified artisan Classicism, free rather than imitative, tempered by the local vernacular, in variations all the way from Surrey to Imperial India.

The Cotswold vernacular was still little understood, and Lutyens never treated it with exaggerated respect. Here he plays with it to create in the glorious hillside setting of Abbotswood his major house in the region. His other larger works are Copse Hill, and the east wing with a billiard room (with plasterwork) and loggia at Miserden Park (1920–21), near Stroud, for F. N. H. Wills – a replacement of one that had been burnt down in 1919.

The original Abbotswood had been built in dull Tudorbethan about 1867, but Lutyens gave it a radical make-over in 1901–02 for Mark Fenwick (1861–1945), a Newcastle banker and member of the Consett Iron Co. Lutyens's new entrance front (north) has a dominant gable to one side, a splendidly bold equilateral triangle with his mannered low eaves almost reaching to the ground. It has quirky fenestration, original and right, and a central rusticated doorway whose segmental pediment answers those – scaled down – above the cross-windows of the upper storeys. The doorway sets the tone for more inventive decoration to the interior in Lutyens's mannered Classical style.

The west front to the fountain garden is one of Lutyens's well-known compositions in his distinctive vernacular Mannerism: two tall gables flank a flat-roofed projecting bay. Its bold pedimented window gives over a rectangular lily pond and pool, aligned on a semi-domed *nympheum* fed from a mask in the keystone by a sparkling jet of water. This composition at the interface between house and garden has been often illustrated, from the contemporary books of Lutyens's biographer, Sir Lawrence Weaver, onwards.

The garden round the house is also by Lutyens, where Gertrude Jekyll's hand is for once notably absent. His design

The north entrance front, Lutyens's major architectural essay in the Cotswolds, with its strong gables and some witty artisan Classical detailing of segmental pediments, and piers answering the rusticated doorway.

of the formal garden is assured and, of course, architectural, with terraced lawns, a canal, pergola, Jacobethan pavilions and loggias. The garden lacks the sense of enclosure and intimacy of Jekyll, and Russell Page described it as 'over mannered'. The client, Fenwick, was a keen and knowledgeable gardener with taste and money, who over a long reign fleshed out the planting scheme and extended the garden less formally into the Victorian parkland to create an imaginative ensemble – the first of the great twentieth-century gardens in the Cotswolds. Lord Redesdale of Batsford Park was full of praise, writing in *Country Life* of February 1913 that Fenwick combined: 'the formality of an Italian architectural garden with the broader and wilder lines of the natural woodland scene, the one fading into the other by the skill of imperceptible gradations.'

The garden has continued to develop, so that it is today better known than the house. Fenwick, crippled by arthritis, went on with undiminished vitality in old age, supervising the design of a rock garden by James Pulham, with a ravine feature over the river Dikler, and planting varieties of heaths and heathers, in muted tones in winter, the woodland garden, an arboretum of specimen trees with a blaze of autumn colours, and numberless alpines and spring bulbs.

Above: *Pergola (now demolished) with the Victorian house behind to the left.*

Left: *The fountain court of 1902 below the west side of the new wing, duplicating one at The Hoo, Sussex, with a long rectangular lily pond.*

Across a sweep of lawn, the spring garden along the valley of the Dikler is memorable, the stream made to tumble over a chain of miniature waterfalls and outcrops of rock, exploiting the site to dramatic effect. The banks were planted with carpets of anemones, primulas, wild orchids, species tulips and a staggering display of fritillaries in spring, flowering shrubs, water- and rock-loving plants, autumn crocuses, with the help of the great garden designer, Russell Page (1906–1985), and the legendary head gardener 'of the old school', Fred Tustin.

Today, under the able guardianship of Robin Scully from Texas, Abbotswood is a place of pilgrimage as a Lutyens garden that has developed into one of the great plantsmen's gardens of the Cotswolds.

Batsford Park, Gloucestershire

Sir (Edward) Guy Dawber (1861–1938) is sometimes known as 'the Lutyens of the West'. He was a contemporary of Gimson and the Barnsleys, and first came to the Cotswolds as Clerk of Works to supervise the construction of Batsford Park (1887–93), near Moreton-in-Marsh, to the designs of the pre-eminent and prolific London practice of Sir Ernest George and Harold Peto. Batsford was a major house for Bertram Freeman-Mitford, later 1st Lord Redesdale, grandfather of the Mitford 'Hons and Rebels', built to replace the earlier Georgian house on the site. The family found it woefully impractical: 'a bugger of a house', recalled one of the Mitford children, Deborah, Duchess of Devonshire, writing to her sister Jessica in 1984.

The style chosen was Elizabethan, to an E-plan, with mullioned and many transomed windows, exaggerated diamond-clustered chimneys, and the inevitable gables of the Cotswold vernacular. Inside there is a baronial, two-storey hall with a staircase gallery, and a huge ballroom. It was the first country house in which Dawber had significant involvement.

He learned the detailing of the local Cotswold vernacular on the job, and the project became a springboard to a lifetime's work as a respected architect working in the Cotswold tradition, always in stone, building well-proportioned houses with a minimum of detailing, which he described as his 'simple and quiet manner'. Mitford, by then Lord Redesdale, introduced Dawber to the neighbouring county gentry, and Dawber in turn enjoyed working for them in the country house tradition. He acknowledged the architects of the Arts and Crafts movement in his earnest study of the vernacular and traditional methods, though his houses depart from the principle of organic truth, as comfortable, convenient and practical, built to indulge his patrons of the Establishment.

Like Lutyens, he developed a fluent Classical style. He remained urbane, and a Londoner at heart, a successful metropolitan professional who ended his career with a knighthood, with none of the Gimson school's interest in 'method', in socialist communitarian ideology and the cult of austerity. He became acknowledged as the expert on the Cotswold vernacular with the publication of *Old Cottages and Farmhouses in the Cotswold District* (1905).

The south front, an essay in Cotswold Neo-Elizabethan, viewed over the terraces, by the fashionable George and Peto partnership, 1887–93. Guy Dawber supervised the execution of the project.

Eyford Park, Gloucestershire

Eyford Park (now Eyford House), near Stow-on-the Wold, is one of Dawber's most successful essays in a light-hearted, Classical manner, handsomely finished with Baroque details and sash windows, built in 1911–12 for John Cheetham. There had been two earlier houses on the estate: the first, was built for the Duke of Shrewsbury in the 1640s, where the poet Milton is said to have penned verses of *Paradise Lost*; the second was an Italianate mansion of the 1870s.

Dawber's replacement house is superbly sited in a hillside setting, on a terrace at the edge of woods near the top of the North Cotswolds. The north entrance front has a symmetrical façade of five bays in ashlar, with a central doorway under a swan-necked pediment, aligned on pairs of pillars, a Dawber mannerism set like dissociated gate piers. Above the doorway is an oculus window framed with swags.

The garden front to the south has a recessed centre, with three, giant, Ionic pilasters, and flanking wings with hipped roofs. The estate was acquired by Sir Cyril and Lady Kleinwort (of Sezincote) in their retirement, who commissioned Graham Stuart Thomas to rework the garden in 1976, with southerly views overlooking the terraces, ha-ha and a serpentine lake. The house is now lived in by their daughter.

Above: *Reciprocal view to the summer house through a theatrical recession of planes, with the garden reordered by Graham Stuart Thomas after 1976.*

Left: *The north front, with piers, is quietly sophisticated with the swan-necked pediment and swags over the central bull's eye; Guy Dawber in his vernacular Classical mode, 1911–12.*

Nether Swell Manor, Gloucestershire

Nether Swell Manor, near Stow-on-the-Wold, is another Dawber house, in a more cluttered and restless Jacobethan vernacular, making reference to nearby Upper Swell Manor. It stands alone down a long drive, with a riot of gabled roofs, oriels and bays, and, after a century of weathering, the main front is a convincing Cotswold-manor fraud. It was built for Sir Walter Douglas Scott in two phases. At first the main house of 1902 was quite small and sparse, built in rubble quarried on the estate, with freestone dressings and double-bay windows with pierced strapwork. It was elevated in a much grander statement, rambling with bold Neo-Renaissance additions of 1909, including a tower and storeyed porch.

Sir Walter, the builder of Nether Swell, was the younger brother of Sir John Murray Scott, the private secretary to Sir William Wallace who set up the Wallace Collection in Hertford House, London. In his day, the garden was ornamented with statuary from the Château de Bagatelle in the Bois de Boulogne, and the house stuffed with art works, tapestries, Sèvres porcelain, and sculpture inherited from Lady Wallace – all dispersed in 1933. There were French interiors, in part surviving, with plasterwork by Marcel Boulanger in the Wallace style, and a Rococo study and Louis XVI dining room with furniture to match.

As with many large houses, the main house has recently been divided into five dwellings, and eight new houses have been built in a walled garden created on the footprint of ugly science blocks, which stood to the rear, dating to the house's post-war use as a Spartan prep school named Hill Place.

Above: *The approach to the main house of 1902 in plain rubble quarried from the estate by Guy Dawber; the Renaissance porch and feudal tower behind were added in a more robust style in 1909.*

Right: *Dawber's scholarly Cotswold vernacular, with canted bays and strapwork parapets, diamond-clustered chimney-stacks and Neo-Renaissance niche with a bronze statue.*

Above: *View from the front porch, with a bronze Mercury. Much of the statuary came from the Château de Bagatelle, near Paris.*

Right: *Staircase hall in 1910, when the house was filled with the art works of the connoisseur and collector Sir Walter Douglas Scott.*

Hilles, Gloucestershire

Detmar Jellings Blow (1867–1939) was, like Dawber, a gentleman-architect, who grew away from an early enthusiasm for Cotswold vernacular, having absorbed it until it was second nature. He was descended from the seventeenth-century organist and composer John Blow, the friend and teacher of England's 'divine genius' (as Gerard Manley Hopkins praised him), Henry Purcell. He had been a contemporary of Lutyens at the Royal College of Art. He was a flamboyant and romantic character, who had stumbled upon Ruskin by chance as a student, while he was sketching at Abbeville Cathedral in northern France. He finished his education under the spell of the great art critic, becoming one of his last acolytes and accompanying him on his final Venetian tour. Blow worked briefly with Ernest Gimson, and began practising in the idealised medieval tradition of the 'wandering architect', living the 'simple life' and moving from one project to the next at the head of his trusted team of masons and craftsmen.

Above: *Hilles (1914–22) from the south west, with its low bay window overlooking the Berkeley Vale.*
Left: *View over the terrace from the central garden porch.*

At first he cultivated the romantic-socialist pose of the Arts and Crafts artist *maudit*, as a friend of William Holman Hunt, Burne-Jones, and Morris's architect, Philip Webb. He worked with Webb on the repair of East Knoyle church in Wiltshire. Webb was the architect of Clouds nearby, his major country house and the great seat of Percy Wyndham. Blow the extrovert and appealing performer was soon taken up with enthusiasm by 'The Souls', both by the Wyndhams at Clouds and, in the Cotswolds, by the Charteris family at Stanway. More genuinely than Dawber, Blow became a well-connected and popular society architect, consorting on equal terms with the landed establishment, a position consolidated following his marriage to the forceful Winifred Tollemache, from Helmingham in Suffolk.

Detmar Blow is exceptional in the Arts and Crafts canon for the assured grandeur of his commissions: completing new mansions, and restoring and extending old ones, with a sure and fluent touch, at the whim of aristocratic patrons. He had genuine sensitivity to the Cotswold vernacular, a sense of scale, materials and texture, adapting it gloriously to his clients' manifold needs in panelling, plasterwork and the confident use of stone. He worked as a committee member

Above: *Hallway with the ceiling in pine boards inserted after a fire, and (beyond) the Burne-Jones's* Primavera *tapestry.*

Right: *Detmar Jellings Blow (1867–1939), owner and architect, by Augustus John.*

Opposite: *Down the wide stairs to the hallway.*

DIEU ET
MON
DROIT

for the Society of the Protection of Ancient Buildings in 1908, restoring the Baroque villa of Bramham in Yorkshire for the Lane Fox family, which had been damaged by fire in 1828.

By 1914, Blow had achieved the security – and the means – to start on his own dream country house, Hilles, at Harescombe, outside Painswick. The house is perched like a look-out on plummeting terraces on the edge of the Cotswolds, with sideways views west over the Berkeley Vale into Wales, today intersected by the motorway below. Here Blow lived out his bohemian ideal as a Fabian utopian, as the family sat down a little awkwardly, one supposes, to kitchen meals at a scrubbed deal table alongside his servants, tenants and craftsmen. Gervase Jackson-Stops in *Country Life* described how the Blows 'created the perfect rural community which breathed Morris's principles of romantic socialism.'

The original L-plan house has a long, almost symmetrical, wing facing south. It ramified as he prospered from his architectural practice with gables and bold bay windows, round headed, then a low tower to the north, when he extended it piecemeal after 1922. The original thatched roof was destroyed in a fire in 1948, and replaced in less appealing stone. The interior is dominated by the big hall with a Morris carpet, and the long room with Mortlake tapestries and Lavery's sensitive little portrait of Winifred Blow. Some rooms have Jacobean detailing, with gloomy oak furniture; others are more delicately textured, furnished with Burne-Jones's *Primavera* tapestry, for example, and four-poster beds, Georgian furniture, family portraits: the composer John Blow by John Riley; Detmar Blow with tousled curls by Augustus John.

A three-arched memorial to Detmar and Winifred Blow stands, uncompleted, at the top of Cud Hill, on the ridge a little way from the house.

The long room with Mortlake tapestries. A Classical screen with a rhythm of fluted columns forms a partition from the big hall.

THE TWENTIETH CENTURY AND BEYOND

The Cotswold ideal, with its architecture and landscape, is part of the cultural history of the twentieth century, with its deep-seated nostalgia and resistance to the tide of inevitable change. After the onset of the Industrial Revolution in 1870 had destroyed the old sense of community, the Cotswolds became in so much of the literature of the twentieth century, in the wake of *Country Life* and the Arts and Crafts movement, a place of escape, away from the degrading influence of the cash nexus. It would be salutary to pretend that the story of the Cotswold house has not quite come to an end, and that the post-war period has spawned worthy successors in a range of styles, continuing to renew and reinvent the vernacular. Examples of solid integral designs are legion, if not in the grand aristocratic tradition.

Above: *The Orchard Room at Highgrove House by Charles Morris of 1997–98: inventive play with elements of the Cotswold vernacular.*

Left: *View of the west garden at Highgrove. The plain house of 1796 was rebuilt following a fire in 1893, with a 'facelift' of pilasters and balustrades added to a scheme of Felix Kelly in 1987. The terrace, with a magnificent cedar by the house, leads across pleached hornbeams to yew battlements in the foreground shaped by Sir Roy Strong.*

If the Cotswolds resisted the precepts of the International Modern Movement, even in diluted form, it was with an instinct for the preservation of the past. Exceptions are isolated. John Campbell was one architect working in the Cotswolds between the wars, who rather unusually had practised many years in Germany, imbuing the philosophy and practice of Modernism before settling near Stroud. An example is the Bear Inn of Rodborough, where in 1925 he added a round corner tower, with an eerie Bavarian feeling. After the War, there are little-known Modernist oddities. Both Broadbridge Mill, near Ozleworth, and Upper Kilcott, near Hillesley, were remodelled for his own occupation by Berthold Lubetkin (1901–1990) after his retirement in 1951; the style sits uneasily in the Cotswolds, where this architect, sometimes described as the most important figure in the British Modernist movement, is popularly remembered as the architect of the Penguin Pool at London Zoo.

Today, the Cotswold vernacular lives on in numerous new buildings, and adaptations to old ones, and traditional building skills have enjoyed something of a revival, more self-conscious and academic. New initiatives in craft training and building crafts skills, led by such prime movers as the Prince of Wales through his Prince's Foundation and the Woodchester Mansion Trust, have become influential forces, planning the country's first Heritage Training Academy.

There have been additions to old houses (from subterranean service rooms at Daneway to a Neo-Georgian façade at Upton House), and so-called 'enabling' development (Northwick Park, Stout's Hill, Highnam), or interpretation centres (Snowshill), as well as demolitions of Victorian and Edwardian offices and servants' wings (Burn's wing at Stanway in 1948–49, and Brandon's wing at Williamstrip in 1946), and improvements for the deprivations of post-war, largely servantless, living (Wormington Grange, reduction and replanning in 1947; Bruern Abbey, demolitions, alterations and external remodelling in three phases from 1956).

The process continues. Planning permission was granted in 2006, after a long battle with conservationists, to demolish the large side wings of 1873 at Barrington Park and permit 'restoration of the house to its original eighteenth-century form.' Great estates continue to adapt old buildings. One of the most successful has been at Badminton, where The Cottage was remodelled as a dower house for David and Lady Caroline Somerset (later the 11th Duke and Duchess of Beaufort), with the addition of a large library with French windows in the 1960s by the architects Sutton, Griffin and Morgan.

There are also dignified translations from the Classical in the style of the late twentieth-century Neo-Georgian. Among the most successful exercises in 'radical classicism' are two by masters in the genre, Quinlan and Francis Terry. Waverton House, near Sezincote (1978–80), is a stud farm, built for Jocelyn Hambro. It perpetuates the stone vernacular of the Cotswolds to a Classical plan, incorporating the stabling in low extending wings in the tradition of the Palladian rural villa-farm; the whole is raised up elegantly on a balustraded platform. The proportions of plan and sections throughout are governed by whole numbers. The Classical details of the exterior are simplified, with plain, unmoulded architraves, using the bolder expression not of Palladio, but of architects such as Michele Sanmicheli. Inside is a single central stairway

Left (above): *Waverton House, near Sezincote, by Quinlan and Francis Terry, 1978–80.*
(below): *The top-lit stairway was contributed by the local firm, Rathbones of Kingham.*
Right: *Hidcote Manor, near Chipping Campden. Looking from the house to the pair of pavilions which draw the eye into the stilt garden of pleached hornbeams laid out after 1915.*

of imperial grandeur, top-lit, with ironwork by Rathbones of Kingham, and decorations by Colefax and Fowler.

Court Farm at Bibury (1986–88), also by Quinlan and Francis Terry, has long, low elevations, of five wide bays on the main front, seven narrower ones to the rear; and a strong central bay with Serliana and statuary. It sits modestly in its village setting, unnoticed, recalling native prototypes, elevated to the standards of the robust Elizabethan Classicism of Robert Smythson.

Cotswold Gardens

The chief glory of the late twentieth century in the Cotswolds, however, lies in the gardens which many great houses have extended, improved, or reordered, often in sympathy with their own historic architecture. The Cotswold garden, like the Cotswold house, has won worldwide acclamation, and, in a region that never wants for superlatives, Timothy Mowl argues that the limestone belt can lay claim to the best group of gardens in England. This is less because it is favoured by micro-climate or soil type, than because of the numerous skilled amateur practitioners living there, among them the great women gardeners of the post-war period: Avilde Lees-Milne at Alderley Grange and Rosemary Verey at Barnsley House, who became hugely influential through their books, their circle of friends and acolytes, and later their consultancy.

The Cotswolds has a group of unrivalled Arts and Crafts gardens, at Hidcote, Kiftsgate, Snowshill and Rodmarton Manor. Of these, Hidcote, perhaps, has been the most influential of all since its first appearance in *Country Life* in 1930, and was the first garden to be taken into the care of the National Trust in 1948, since when it has been beautifully presented and managed. It was the creation of a naturalised American, Lawrence Johnston, who bought Hidcote Bartrim Manor in 1907. He started to lay out the gardens, aligned on an access parallel to the house, from about 1910, creating a series of rooms defined by hedges and walls – each with a different colour-theme – and with linking vistas. The garden, with its stilt hedges in hornbeam, box parterres and open lawns bounded by yews, is renowned for its rare trees and shrubs and planting.

Barnsley House was inherited by David and Rosemary Verey in 1958, an architectural historian and a garden designer

Above: *Barnsley House, near Cirencester. The south front of 1697 with the garden developed by David and Rosemary Verey showing the walk of Irish yews, with open lawns and herbaceous planting.*

Left: *Hidcote Manor, near Chipping Campden. Reciprocal view from the stilt garden towards the house.*

and writer respectively, early in their married life. They started laying out a plantsman's garden with a sure sense of architecture, introducing many historical motifs derived from wide reading and reflection in classical horticultural literature: a bibliophile's garden.

There are knot parterres after John Parkinson's *Paradisi in sole: paradisus terrestris* (1656), a lime and golden laburnum walk, a *potager* reminiscent of the French Neo-Classical garden with balls of privet and brick paths, a walk of Irish yews – all of which have created influential precedents imitated since in numerous other gardens. The colours are muted as a Dutch flower painting. Sculpture, early pieces by Simon and Judith Verity, provides focal points: a veiled hunting lady, a frog fountain supporting butting Cotswold rams, and two dwarf gardeners of the Veneto. A sundial has an inscription in italic quoted from John Evelyn, with its hint of Paradise to come: '*As no man be very miserable that is Master of Garden here, so will no man ever be happy who is not sure of a garden hereafter*'.

Highgrove, the family home of the Prince of Wales and the Duchess of Cornwall, was in its origins a house often attributed to one of the region's most successful late-Georgian architects, Anthony Keck, of King's Stanley, for the mill owner John Paul Paul. The original house, dated 1793–96, was gutted by fire a century later, in 1893, and rebuilt the following year, this time as a simplified late Victorian box to a comfortable but undistinguished, broadly Georgian, design.

Highgrove was acquired with its (then) small estate by the Duchy of Cornwall for the occupation of the Prince of Wales in 1980. The Prince asked Felix Kelly to 'improve' on the exterior, and the artist produced a fantasy sketch in 1985. A sense of 'sweetness and light' hangs on the main elevations, now enclosed in a cage of pilasters, with upstanding balustrading, pediment and urn finials to enrich the roofscape in a manner more country Baroque than Neo-Classical. The design was worked on and realised by Peter Falconer of Minchinhampton, a post-war gentleman-architect (who worked on my own house), in 1987. The result has been a happy enlivening of a staid design.

But the undisputed glory of Highgrove today is the garden. The Prince of Wales inherited a blank canvas save for depleted shelterbelts and a banal walk of golden yews marching from the terrace into the landscape, set on a rather unpromising level site of thin stony soils without views, and by a road.

The transformation has been complete, embodying his gardening ideals and organic principles. Now it is embellished with wooden temples and primitive huts by Julian and Isabel Bannerman set in a sacred grove, apt inscriptions (one from Horace, mediated by Montaigne, reads: '*virtutem verba putant, lucum lignam*', from *Epistles*, VI), a meditation room or 'sanctuary', incorporating Keith Critchlow's Neo-Platonic sacred geometry, Orthodox icons set among *gunnera*, Neo-Rococo conceits such as root houses, a stumpery planted with hostas, ferns and hellebores, a whimsical pigeon house in Cotswold stone, arbours and seats, and pools. There is statuary throughout, a copy of the bronze gladiator from Wilton, busts of the owner and his admired friends (one recalls Kathleen Raine, another Miriam Rothschild), a nude sylvan goddess. And planting curious and cunning.

The planting was undertaken with the advice of gardening gurus. Molly, Lady Salisbury (of Hatfield and Cranborne) was involved with an early project: the sundial garden of 1981–82, connecting to the south front, in black and white, hedged in by yews. Rosemary Verey planted the cottage garden, free form with serpentine paths, but her genius presides elsewhere. For instance, the walled kitchen, recalling the *potager* at Barnsley, transforms the utilitarian with formal pergolas and tunnels of arching apple trees, and crossing paths, roses and aromatic plants – all the product of a good deal of labour. Topiary is shaped to Renaissance forms of sweeping battlements by the hands and shears of Sir Roy Strong. Dame Miriam Rothschild, the 'Queen Bee' naturalist and entomologist, scattered seeds of wild flowers in the meadows. Despite a committed post-modern Internationalism, its sacred grove and the meditation halls, which are the *locus amoenus* of a prince in the tradition of Lorenzo de Medici and his philosopher Ficino, Highgrove is still at heart a Cotswold garden, continuing the insights of Rosemary Verey into a new millennium and constantly evolving.

An Islamic carpet garden is a recent addition, quite un-Cotswold, a walled sanctuary animated with water reflected in rills and myrtle pools, or playing in a marble bowl sculpted into sixty-four lobed segments. The rich textures of *azulejos* and mosaics sparkle with colour by sunken beds along the cross walks, planted with delphiniums and citrus trees; a recreation of paradise garden traditions found from the Alhambra to Isphahan.

One of the Prince of Wales's recent projects is the Orchard Room by Charles Morris of Norfolk, dated 1997–98. It is of course not a country house, but a utilitarian annexe to one, a single-storey enclosure for versatile spaces, which adapt as tearooms, a conference and reception room, shop, lavatories, and offices. These are the amenities typical of a country house open to the public in the twenty-first century, but everything here is furnished and finished with princely taste and wit – a figure sculpture by Nicholas Dimbleby in low relief, rugs and textiles gathered on travels in the East.

It is domestic in scale, a garden pavilion fronting a paved courtyard, and inventive in its play with the elements of the Cotswold vernacular. There are stone-tiled roofs, rendered walls (limewashed, of course), fat stumpy columns like those in local market halls at Tetbury and Dursley, and plasterwork by Steve Welsh. The cross-gables are reduced in proportion, standing back from the strong wooden eaves cornice, which functions as a gutter all round the building.

The Orchard Room represents a moment in the unfolding story of the Cotswolds, built in stone, drawing on vernacular traditions, but telling a particularly late-twentieth-century story about the attractions and pleasures associated with this region, rightly celebrated as the quintessence of Englishness.

Left: *Highgrove House, reflected in the stone pool. The west garden has a thyme walk flanked by an axis of golden yews, now formally sculpted, virtually all that remains from the garden taken over by HRH The Prince of Wales in 1980.*

Below: *A garden seat on a raised platform at Highgrove: a hidden enclosure in the Arts and Crafts manner.*

SELECT BIBLIOGRAPHY

Atkyns, the Younger, Sir Robert, *The Ancient and Present State of Glostershire*, 1712; 2nd ed. 1768; reissued, new intro by B. S. Smith, E. P. Publishing, Wakefield, 1974.

Baker, Oliver, *In Shakespeare's Warwickshire and the Unknown Years*, Simpkin Marshall, London, 1937.

Bigland, Sir Ralph, *Historical, Monumental and Genealogical Collections Relative to the County of Gloucestershire*, 1786 (1st ed.); new edition, ed. B. S. Smith, (4 vols), Bristol and Gloucestershire Archaeological Society, Gloucester, 1989–95.

Bray, Jean, *The Lady of Sudeley*, Sutton Publishing, Stroud, 2004.

Brewer, J. N., with engravings by Storer, J. and H. S., *Delineations of Gloucestershire: being Views of the Principal Seats of the Nobility and Gentry*, Sherwood, Gilbert and Piper, London, 1825–27.

Brill, Edith, *Life and Tradition in the Cotswolds*, Dent, London, 1973.

Cooke, R., *West Country Houses*, Clifton, 1957.

Cooper, Nicholas, *The Jacobean Country House: From the Archives of Country Life*, Aurum Press, London, 2006.

Cox, J. C., *Gloucestershire: Little Guide*, Methuen & Co. London, 1914; revised by H. Stratton-Davis, Methuen & Co., London, 1949.

Crossley, Alan, Hassall, Tom, and Salway, Peter, *William Morris's Kelmscott: Landscape and History*, Windgather Press, Oxford, 2007.

Dawber, E. Guy, *Old Cottages, Farm-houses and other Stone Buildings in the Cotswold District*, B. T. Batsford, London, 1905.

Delderfield, E. R., *West Country Historic Houses and their Families: The Cotswold Area*, vol 3, David & Charles, Newton Abbot, 1973.

Ditchfield, Peter Hampson, *The Manor Houses of England*, B. T. Batsford, London, 1910.

Drury, Michael, *Wandering Architects*, Shaun Tyas, Stamford, 2000.

Evans, Herbert A., *Highways and Byways in Oxford and the Cotswolds*, Macmillan, London, 1905.

Finberg, H. P. R. (ed.), *Gloucestershire Studies*, Leicester University Press, 1957.

Fosbroke, Thomas Dudley, *Abstracts of Records and Manuscripts Respecting the County of Gloucester, Formed into a History*, (2 vols), 1807.

Gibbs, J. Arthur, *A Cotswold Village*, John Murray, London, 1898.

Harris, John, *Badminton: The Duke of Beaufort, His House*, 2007.

Hussey, Christopher, *English Country Houses: Early Georgian, 1715–1760*, Country Life, London, 1955; (revised, 1965).

—, *English Country Houses: Mid-Georgian, 1760–1800*, Country Life, London, 1956.

—, *English Country Houses: Late Georgian, 1800–1840*, Country Life, London, 1958.

Jewson, Norman, *By Chance I did Rove*, Cirencester, 1951.

Kholucy, S., Kerr, I. M., Powers, A., Ramsden, G., Smith, E., Watts, V., Young, R., *A View of the Cotswolds*, Whittington Press, Andoversford, 2005.

Kingsley, Nicholas, *The Country Houses of Gloucestershire* Vol. I, 1500–1750, Cheltenham, 1989; revised ed., Phillimore, Chichester, 2001.

—, Vol. II, 1660–1830, Phillimore, Chichester, 1992.

—, and Hill, Michael, Vol. III, 1830–2000, Phillimore, Chichester, 2001.

Lees-Milne, James, *Some Cotswold Country Houses*, Dovecote Press, Wimborne, 1987.

Lethaby, W. R., Powell, A., and Griggs, F. L., *Ernest Gimson: His Life and Work*, Shakespeare Head Press, 1924; (facsimile ed., 20th-Century Publishing, 2006).

Leyland, John, (ed.), *Gardens Old and New: the Country House and its Garden Environment*, Country Life, London, 1907.

Lysons, Revd. Samuel, *A Collection of Gloucestershire Antiquities*, 1803.

Mander, Nicholas, *Owlpen Manor: a short history and guide*, Owlpen, 2006.

Massingberd, H. Montgomery, *English Manor Houses*, Laurence King, London, 2001.

Massingham, H. J., *Cotswold Country: A Survey of Limestone England from the Dorset Coast to Lincolnshire*, B. T. Batsford, London, 1937.

Morris, William, *News from Nowhere*, 1890.

Mowl, Timothy, *Historic Gardens of Gloucestershire*, Tempus Publishing, Stroud, 2002.

Musson, Jeremy, *The English Manor House: From the Archives of Country Life*, Aurum Press, London, 1999; (pb 2007).

Robinson, W. J., *West Country Manors*, St Stephen's Press, Bristol, 1930.

Rodwell, Kirsty, and Bell, Robert, *Acton Court: The Evolution of an Early Tudor Courtier's House*, English Heritage, London, 2004.

Rudder, Samuel, *A New History of Gloucestershire*, Cirencester, 1779; reissued by Alan Sutton, Stroud, 1977, 1986.

Smyth, John, *The Berkeley Manuscripts*, ed. Sir John Maclean, (3 vols), Bristol and Gloucestershire Archaeological Society, Gloucester, 1883–85.

Talbot, R., and Whiteman, R., *Cotswold Landscapes*, Weidenfeld and Nicolson, London, 1999.

Tipping, H. Avray, *English Homes*, (9 vols), B. T. Batsford, London, 1921–37.

—, *The English Renaissance House*, Country Life, London, 1912.

Verey, David, *Gloucestershire: A Shell Guide*, revised ed., Faber & Faber, London, 1970.

—, *Gloucestershire: The Cotswolds*, Buildings of England series (2nd ed.) Penguin Books, London, 1979; 3rd ed., revised by Alan Brooks, Yale University Press, London, 1999.

The Victoria History of the County of Gloucester, (1st vol) 1907.

Wales, HRH the Prince of, and Lycett-Green, Candida, *The Garden at Highgrove*, Weidenfeld and Nicolson, London, 2001.

Wood-Jones, Raymond, *Traditional Domestic Architecture in the Banbury Region*, Manchester University Press, 1963.

INDEX

Page numbers in *italics* refer to illustrations